# THE CASE FOR
# Islamo-Christian Civilization

## Richard W. Bulliet

COLUMBIA UNIVERSITY PRESS

NEW YORK

COLUMBIA UNIVERSITY PRESS
*Publishers Since 1893*
New York, Chichester, West Sussex
Copyright © 2004 Columbia University Press
All rights Reserved

Library of Congress Cataloging-in-Publication Data
Bulliet, Richard W.
 The case for Islamo-Christian civilization /
Richard W. Bulliet.
  p.  cm.
 Includes bibliographical references and index.
 ISBN 0–231–12796–0 (cloth : alk. paper)
  1. Civilization, Islamic.  2. Civilization, Christian.
3. Islam—21st century.  I. Title.
DS36.85.B85 2004
303.48'2176701821—dc22

                                    2004041314

Columbia University Press books are printed
on permanent and durable acid-free paper
Printed in the United States of America

c 10 9 8 7 6 5 4 3 2 1

References to Internet Web Sites (URLs) were
accurate at the time of writing. Neither the author
nor Columbia University Press is responsible for
Web sites that may have expired or changed since
the book was prepared

*Designed by Lisa Hamm*

# Contents

# Preface

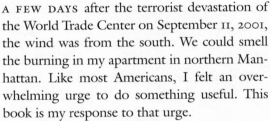

A FEW DAYS after the terrorist devastation of the World Trade Center on September 11, 2001, the wind was from the south. We could smell the burning in my apartment in northern Manhattan. Like most Americans, I felt an overwhelming urge to do something useful. This book is my response to that urge.

Though it is based on my career as a professor, this is not a scholarly book in the purest sense. My hope is that the different perspectives I am proposing will appeal not just to specialists but to many different audiences. The four chapters it contains do not add up to a continuous historical exposition, but they all contribute to the idea that the title of the book is intended to evoke: Despite the enmity that has often divided them, Islam and the West have common roots and share much of their history. Their confrontation today arises not from essential differences, but from a long and willful determination to deny their kinship.

The first chapter grew out of a speculative essay I wrote around 1970—and filed away with the thought that certain ideas are so large that they are best published by old men with white beards. I now have a white beard and am approaching old age faster than I care to admit. The ideas in the second chapter began to gestate a few years later when it first dawned on me that the return of Islam as a political force was not only the most important contemporary development in the Muslim world, but one that had clear, and indeed necessary, historical causes. The Iranian revolution confirmed these hunches a few years later, and I have been deeply interested in Islamic politics ever since. The third chapter is rooted both in my student years in the fledgling field of Middle East Studies, and in my experiences with the Middle East Studies Association, of which I was Executive Secretary from 1977 to 1981. The fourth chapter takes its inspiration and title from a book I published in 1994.

I have received helpful comments on the text from several people to whom I owe a deep debt of gratitude: Mark Bulliet, Lucy Bulliet, Mohsen Ashtiany, Lisa Anderson, Ze'ev Magen, and Mia Bloom.

Richard W. Bulliet
March 2004

THE CASE FOR

# Islamo-Christian Civilization

*The past and future of the West cannot be fully compre-
hended without appreciation of the twinned relationship
it has had with Islam over some fourteen centuries. The
same is true of the Islamic world.*

CHAPTER I

# The Case for Islamo-Christian Civilization

AWESOME POWER resides in the terms we
employ. Harvard professor Samuel Huntington's use of the phrase "Clash of Civilizations"
as the title of an article in *Foreign Affairs* in
1993 illustrates this truth. Pundits and scholars
immediately sorted themselves out as supporters or critics of Huntington's phraseology, as
often as not basing their opinions more on the
rhetoric of the title than on the specifics of his
argument. By wielding these three words at a
propitious moment, and under respected auspices, Huntington shifted a discourse of Middle East confrontation that had been dominated by nationalist and Cold War rhetoric since
the days of Gamal Abdel Nasser in the 1950s
and 1960s. The new formulation took on almost cosmic proportions: the Islamic religion,
or more precisely the world Muslim community that professes that religion, versus contemporary Western culture, with its Christian,
Jewish, and secular humanist shadings. How

quickly and fatefully a well-chosen phrase can challenge perceptions of reality.

In all fairness, it must be recognized that Huntington imputes no particular religious notions to the "Islamic civilization" he sees as fated to confront the West in the twenty-first century. His argument focuses on comparing an idealized "Western civilization," based on democracy, human rights, free enterprise, and globalization, with economic, social, and political structures in other parts of the world that he sees as unsympathetic, adversarial, and incapable of betterment. This line of thought does not differ greatly from the theories of global progress toward modernity, as exemplified by the contemporary West, that were popular in the quarter century following World War II. However, Huntington's version corrects a shortcoming of those earlier "modernization" theories. In the 1950s and 1960s theorists commonly opined that modernization would relegate religion to an insignificant role in public affairs. But the surge of Islamic political activism that hit a first crest in the Iranian Revolution of 1979 showed the hollowness of these predictions and thus opened the way for Huntington to reintroduce a religious terminology, albeit one barren of religious elaboration, into a more pessimistic prediction of future developments.

It is hard to strip religious terms of religious content, however. The "Islamic civilization" in Huntington's "Clash of Civilizations" has been understood religiously, at least some of the time, by defenders and detractors alike. Coincidentally, the same phrase appeared in a book title in 1926: *Young Islam on Trek: A Study in the Clash of Civilizations*.[1] Its author, Basil Mathews, was Literature Secretary in the World's Alliance of YMCA's, but his vision of Islam, similar to many others of the same period, would strike many of Huntington's admirers as being right up-to-date.

The system [*i.e.*, Islam] is, indeed, in essence military. The creed is a war-cry. The reward of a Paradise of maidens for those who die in battle, and loot for those who live, and the joy of battle and domination thrills the tribal Arab. The discipline of prayer five times a day is a drill. The muezzin cry from the minaret is a bugle-call. The equality of the Brotherhood gives the equality and *esprit de corps* of the rank and file of the army. The Koran is army orders. It is all clear, decisive, ordained—men fused and welded by the fire and discipline into a single sword of conquest.[2]

Can we have a liberalized Islam? Can Science and the Koran agree? . . . Conviction grows that the reconciliation is not possible. Islam really liberalized is simply a non-Christian Unitarianism. It ceases to be essential Islam. It may believe in God; but He is not the Allah of the Koran and Mohammed is not his Prophet; for it cancels the iron system that Mohammed created.[3]

Huntington's partisans—except for the evangelical Christians among them—would not see eye to eye with Mathews on everything. As a missionary, Mathews expressed a firm conviction that Protestant Christianity could be what he calls "a Voice that will give [young Muslims] a Master Word for living their personal lives and for building a new order of life for their lands." His criticism of the West oddly echoes some of the voices of the Muslim revival, suggesting that this sort of criticism can take root in other than Muslim soil:

Western civilization can never lead them to that goal. Obsessed by material wealth, obese with an industrial plethora, drunk with the miracles of its scientific advance, blind to the riches of the world of the spirit, and deafened to the inner Voice by the outer clamor, Western civilization may destroy the old in Islam, but it cannot fulfill the new.

When the shriek of the factory whistle has drowned the voice of the muezzin, and when the smoke-belching chimney has dwarfed the minaret, obscured the sky, and poisoned the air, young Islam will be no nearer to the Kingdom of God. Their bandits will simply forsake the caravan routes of the desert for the safer and more lucrative mercantile and militarist fields.

Nor can the churches of Christendom, as they are today and of themselves, lead the Moslem peoples to that goal. Limited in their vision, separative in spirit, tied to ecclesiastical systems, the churches of themselves if transported *en bloc* to the Moslem world, would not save it. They have not saved their own civilization. They have not made Christian their own national foreign policies in relation to the Moslem peoples. They have not purged the Western commerce that sells to the East and that grows rich on its oil-wells, but passes by on the other side while the Armenian, stripped and beaten, lies in the ditch of misery.[4]

I do not mean to suggest by these citations that Huntington borrowed either his title or his ideas, much less his writing style, from Mathews. The little-remembered YMCA worthy was giving voice to the standard Protestant missionary rhetoric of his time. Huntington's espousal of secular Western values substitutes pugnacity and pessimism for Mathews' optimism and religious zeal. (Indeed, Mathews' choice of title plays off of, and energizes, the much better known book title by Arnold Toynbee published three years before: *The Western Question in Greece and Turkey: A Study in the Contact of Civilizations*.[5]) For all their differences, however, the coincidental employment of the same phrase for essentially the same subject shows that the anxiety many American observers of the Muslim world have felt ever since the Iranian Revolution is not entirely new. Protestant missionaries, who outnumbered any other group of Americans in non-Western lands and accounted for the great preponderance of American thought about Asia and Africa prior to World War II, harbored an ill-disguised contempt for Islam that looms in the background of today's increasingly vitriolic debates about Islam and the West.

Huntington's recoining of the phrase "Clash of Civilizations" successfully captured an array of feelings that had been calling out for a slogan ever since Khomeini toppled the Shah from his throne. Other phrases—"Crescent of Crisis," "Arc of Instability," "Islamic Revolution"—had auditioned for the part with indifferent success. No one much disagreed, at least at the level of vagueness that informs most foreign policy posturing, about what it was that needed a name; but compressing it into a single phrase proved difficult. "Clash of Civilizations" caught the imagination because it was dynamic, interactive, innocent in Huntington's exposition of awkward definitions and boundaries, not transparently bigoted or racist, and vaguely Hegelian in the seeming profundity of its dialectical balance between good and evil. Combined with its author's eminence as a noted political scientist, and the reputation for sagacious insight commonly ascribed to *Foreign Affairs* by its subscribers, "Clash of Civilizations" won the prize.

Beyond its surface attraction, however, lay a deeper allure harking back to Basil Mathews' era. Civilizations that are destined to clash cannot seek together a common future. Like Mathews' Islam, Huntington's Islam is beyond redemption. The book on Islam is closed. The strain of Protestant American thought that both men are heir to, pronounces against Islam the same self-righteous and unequivocal sentence of "otherness" that American Protestants once visited upon Catholics and Jews.

The comparison with Protestant views about Catholics and Jews is worth pursuing. Whatever became of the ferocious Protestant refusal to visualize an American future—the future that has actually transpired—in which Protestants and Catholics would agree to disagree on selected matters, but otherwise live in harmony and mutual respect? Symbolically, John F. Kennedy's 1960 victory in the Democratic primary in largely Protestant West Virginia proved that the American people had a greater capacity for inclusion than their preachers and theologians did. How about the Protestant anti-Semitism that severely constricted the residential, educational, and occupational options of American Jews and permitted a virulent hater like Henry Ford to be viewed as a great man? From the 1950s onward, with the reality of the Holocaust and the ghastly consequences of European anti-Semitism ever more apparent, the term "Judeo-Christian civilization" steadily emerged from an obscure philosophical background—Nietzsche used "Judeo-Christian" scornfully in *The Antichrist* to characterize society's failings—to become the perfect expression of a new feeling of inclusiveness toward Jews, and of a universal Christian repudiation of Nazi barbarism. We now use the phrase almost reflexively in our schoolbooks, our political rhetoric, and our presentation of ourselves to others around the world.

The unquestioned acceptance of "Judeo-Christian civilization" as a synonym for "Western civilization" makes it clear that history is not destiny. No one with the least knowledge of the past two thousand years of relations between Christians and Jews can possibly miss the irony of linking in a single term two faith communities that decidedly did not get along during most of that period. One suspects that a heavenly poll of long-departed Jewish and Christian dignitaries would discover majorities in both camps expressing repugnance for the term.

Substantively, a historian would argue, the term is amply warranted. Common scriptural roots, shared theological concerns, continuous interaction at a societal level, and mutual contributions to what in modern times has become a common pool of thought and feeling give the Euro-American Christian and Jewish communities solid grounds for declaring their civilizational solidarity. Yet the scriptural and doctrinal linkages between Judaism and Christianity are no closer than those between Judaism and Islam, or between Christianity and Islam; and historians are well aware of the enormous contributions of Muslim thinkers to the pool of late medieval philosophical and scientific thought that European Christians and Jews later drew upon to create the modern West. Nor has there been any lack of contact between Islam and the West. Despite periods of warfare, European merchants for centuries carried on a lively commerce with the Muslims on the southern and eastern shores of the Mediterranean; and the European imagination has long teemed with stories of Moors, Saracens, and oriental fantasy. Politically, fourteen of today's thirty-four European countries were at one time or another wholly or partially ruled by Muslims for periods of a century or more. The historians of these countries sometimes characterize these periods of Muslim rule as anomalies, inexplicable gaps in what should have been a continuous Christian past, or as ghastly episodes of unrelenting oppression, usually exemplified by a handful of instances. In reality, however, most of the people who lived under Muslim rule accustomed themselves to the idea, and to the cultural outlook that went with it, and lived peaceable daily lives.

Our current insistence on seeing profound differences between Islam and the West, what Huntington calls civilizational differences, revives a sentiment of great antiquity. As in the past, dramatic events have catalyzed this reawakening. The fall of America's friend, the Shah of Iran, and the anguishing detention of American diplomatic personnel in Tehran in 1979, were but a prelude to the terrorist attacks on the World Trade Center and the Pentagon of September 11, 2001. However, they gave us a twenty-year head start on worrying about Muslims conspiring to carry out violent political acts professedly based on religious principles. Previous cataclysms echo in the background of these events: the fall of Crusader Jerusalem to Saladin in 1187, the fall of Byzantine Constantinople to the Ottomans in 1453, and the nearly successful Ottoman siege of Vienna in 1529 are but three. The aftermath of each of these events brought with it a shudder of horror at what might transpire should the Muslims prevail on a grander scale. The historian Edward Gibbon gave this fear its classical expression in the eighteenth century in his discussion of what might have happened if a Saracen raiding party from Spain had not suffered defeat at the hands of Charles Martel at the Battle of Tours in 732. "Perhaps the interpretation of the Koran would now be taught in the schools of Oxford, and her pupils might demonstrate to a circumcised people the sanctity and truth of the revelation of Mahomet."[6]

Here is how a Lutheran pamphleteer expressed this sentiment in 1537 when many Europeans thought a new and possibly successful siege of Vienna was imminent:

Christians should also take comfort in the knowledge that the Turkish Empire is God's enemy, and that God will not allow it to annihilate the Christians. Although God has caused this empire to arise in these last times as the most severe of punishments, nonetheless He will not allow the Christians to succumb completely, and Mahomet will not rule alone in the whole world . . . Therefore those who fight against the Turk should be confident . . . that their fighting will not be in vain, but will serve to check the Turk's advance, so that he will not become master of all the world.[7]

It may well be that past episodes of Islamophobia did more good than harm. They rallied frightened people and encouraged them to seek refuge from despair in their religious faith, and the military responses they contributed to ideologically were probably no bloodier than they would have been anyway. By good fortune—and Christian antipathy toward foreigners—few Muslims were resident in European Christian lands so there wasn't anyone local to kill when preachers whipped their congregations into an Islamophobic froth. The Jews, of course, had worse luck when the arrow of Christian alarm pointed in their direction, as it did many times, including the time of the Black Death of 1348–1349. "In the matter of this plague, the Jews throughout the world were reviled and accused in all lands of having caused it through the poison which they are said to have put into the water and the wells . . . and for this reason the Jews were burnt all the way from the Mediterranean into Germany."[8]

We are no longer living in medieval isolation, however. Large Muslim minorities reside and work in almost every country in the world, including every European land and the United States and Canada. The potential for tragedy in our current zeal for seeing Islam as a malevolent Other should make us wary of easy formulations that can cleave our national societies into adversarial camps. A number of years ago a government adviser from Belgium visited with a group of scholars at the Middle East Institute of Columbia University. She was looking for ideas on how to induce the Muslims living in Belgium to become more like "normal" citizens. They were more than welcome to live in Belgium, she averred, but surely it would be best if they were distributed a few here and a few there so that they would not constitute a visibly different social group. Their headscarves and beards would not be so noticeable, and they would not perturb the Belgian national community. As we were sitting in a room overlooking Harlem, it was pointed out to her that clustered communities of difference do not always have to be thought of as ghettos. Socially visible minorities are not only a given in American life, but also a wellspring of cultural creativity. Perhaps in time the folks with the headscarves and beards would become a parallel resource for Belgium.

The question confronting the United States is whether the tragedy of September 11 should be an occasion for indulging in the Islamophobia embodied in slogans like "Clash of Civilizations," or an occasion for affirming the principle of inclusion that represents the best in the American tradition. The coming years may see wars and disasters that dwarf what we have already endured. But they must not see the stigmatization of a minority of the American population by an overwrought majority whipped up by the idea that that minority belongs to a different and malign religious civilization. "Clash of Civilizations" must be retired from public discourse before the people who like to use it actually begin to believe it.

## "Islamo-Christian Civilization"

To the best of my knowledge, no one uses, or has ever used, the term "Islamo-Christian civilization." Moreover, I would hazard the guess that many Muslims and Christians will bristle at the very idea it seems to embody, and other readers will look suspiciously at the omission of "Judeo-" from the phrase. I can only hope that they will withhold final judgment until they have considered my "case" for introducing the term.

To begin with, why not "Islamo-Judeo-Christian Civilization"? If I were looking for a term to signal the common scriptural tradition of these three religions, that might be an acceptable, albeit awkward, phrase. But for this purpose, phrases like "Abrahamic religions," "Children of Abraham," and "Semitic scriptualism" do quite well. I am trying to convey something different. The historical basis for thinking of the Christian society of Western Europe—not all Christians everywhere—and the Muslim society of the Middle East and North Africa—not all Muslims everywhere—as belonging to a single historical civilization goes beyond the matter of scriptural tradition. This historic Muslim-Christian relationship also differs markedly from the historic Jewish-Christian relationship that is more hidden than celebrated in the phrase "Judeo-Christian Civilization." European Christians and Jews—no one includes the Jews of Yemen or the Christians of Ethiopia in discussions of "Western" origins—share a history of cohabitation that was more often tragic than constructive, culminating in the horrors of the Holocaust. Cohabitation between Muslims and the Christians of Western Europe has been far less intense. Rather than the unequal sharing of social, political, and physical space underlying the Jewish-Christian relationship in Europe, which may fruitfully be compared with the historic Muslim-Jewish relationship in the Middle East and North Africa, the term "Islamo-Christian civilization" denotes a prolonged and fateful intertwining of sibling societies enjoying sovereignty in neighboring geographical regions and following parallel historical trajectories. Neither the Muslim nor the Christian historical path can be fully understood without relation to the other. While "Judeo-Christian civilization" has specific historical roots *within* Europe and in response to the catastrophes of the past two centuries, "Islamo-Christian civilization" involves different historical and geographical roots and has different implications for our contemporary civilizational anxieties.

Let it also be noted that there are two other hyphenated civilization that deserve discussion, but that will not be discussed here. A treatment of "Judeo-Muslim civilization" would focus on scriptural, legal, and ritual connections between these two faiths; on Jewish communities in Muslim lands and their literatures in

Judaeo-Arabic and Judaeo-Persian; and on the profound intellectual and religious cross-fertilization best represented in the works of Jewish and Muslim thinkers in Islamic Spain. A great deal of scholarly writing has already been devoted to these subjects, though not under the rubric "Judeo-Muslim civilization. The second hyphen would link Islam with Orthodox Christianity in what could be called "Byzantino-Muslim civilization." (Oswald Spengler preferred the term "Magian" in *The Decline of the West*.) Where Latin Christians outside of Spain had little first-hand experience with Muslim society, many Orthodox Christians lived for centuries under discriminatory conditions in Muslim lands. Thus while Muslim thinkers had little contact with intellectual life in Western Europe, they drew heavily on the Greek heritage preserved by Orthodox Christianity. And the various Christian communities of the east entered the modern period with attitudes toward Islam that differed profoundly from those of Western Europe. But that discussion I will leave to other hands.

Before undertaking to argue in support of Islamo-Christian civilization—it is time to drop the quotation marks—the broader implications of using such a term should be made clear. First, its use renders Huntington's "Clash of Civilizations" definitionally nonsensical. If the Muslim societies of the Middle East and North Africa, and the Christian societies of Western Europe and America, are conceived of as belonging to the same civilization, then conflicts between the two constituent elements of that single civilization would automatically take on an internecine character, analogous historically to past conflicts between Catholicism and Protestantism. Whatever the level of hostility between the parties in conflict, the presumption of a common heritage would prevent their being conceived of as different civilizations, and consequently make it easier to imagine their eventual reconciliation. Russia "rejoining" Europe after the fall of the Soviet Union affords a comparison. Blood is thicker than holy water.

Secondly, current inquiries into whether Muslims are capable of rising to the level of Western civilization, or of civilization at all in the minds of some, would become irrelevant. Western critics of Islam persistently propose civilizational litmus tests: Does Islam meet, or is it on its way to meeting, Western standards of gender equality? Can Islam conceive of human rights in a manner that sufficiently resembles Western conceptions to be counted as civilized? Does Muslim understanding of religious toleration and secularism come close enough to Western ideals for inclusion in the civilization club? Tests like these, conceived in willful denial of the appalling failure of most Western societies, as recently as a hundred years ago, to live up to the same standards, are intended as rhetorical devices for finding Islam wanting rather than as serious questions.

Even today, islands of religious practitioners within both Judaism and Christianity profess illiberal views, ranging from limitations on the behavior and life choices of women, to advocacy of government support for religious organizations, to hopes for an imminent messianic theocracy, that depart substantially from the egalitarian and secular standards that the would-be Western crusaders of "The Clash of Civilizations" have emblazoned on their banners. Scarcely any of the unattractive strictures and intolerant attitudes manifested by *some* Muslim groups lack parallels among *some* Christian and Jewish groups, or among *some* post-religious Western secularists, for that matter. But since Jews, Christians, and Western secularists have named themselves as charter members of the civilization club, the ideological or behavioral shortcomings, from the majority's point of view, of this or that Jewish or Christian group do not impugn or threaten the civilizational inclusion of those religious traditions as a whole. Christianity and Judaism pass by definition the civilizational litmus tests proposed for Islam even though some of their practitioners dictate women's dress codes, prohibit alcoholic beverages, demand prayer in public schools, persecute gays and lesbians, and damn members of other faiths to hell. Muslims of every stripe, on the other hand, stand accused of being party, by reason of religious belief, to the worst behaviors manifested by some groups of their coreligionaries. Jim Jones, David Koresh, and Meir Kahane do not typify

Christianity and Judaism in the eyes of civilized West, but those same eyes are prone to see Osama bin Laden and Mullah Muhammad Omar as typifying Islam.

What stands in the way of our conceptualization of an Islamo-Christian civilization is a historical master narrative rooted in fourteen centuries of fear and polemic, and, of course, the current conviction among many Westerners that there is something "wrong" with Islam. I propose first to investigate in some detail the former problem, the age-old master narrative, and reserve the question of what, if anything, went wrong in Islam for my next chapter. If a persuasive case can be made for re-narrating the last fourteen centuries in terms of an Islamo-Christian civilization, it will facilitate an analysis of more recent events in the Middle East and of the current crisis of authority within Islam.

Superficial objections to re-narrating history in this way abound. Here are a few of the obstacles that seem to stand in the way of linking Muslim history with that of Latin Christendom:

- *Chronological discrepancy*: Muhammad lived seven hundred years after Christ.
- *Inveterate hostility*: Islam repeatedly attacked Christendom and has shown unrelenting enmity toward Christians.
- *Christian experience*: The Christians who confronted Islam over the centuries never saw it as anything but an enemy, alien power.
- *Scriptural error*: The many stories shared between the Quran and the Bible are inaccurate or distorted in their Quranic version.
- *Denial of divine truth*: Islam's recognition of Abraham, Moses, Jesus, and Muhammad as Messengers of God stops short of affirming Christ's divinity.
- *Ingratitude*: Islam has never recognized its doctrinal debt to Judaism and Christianity and has never accepted them as parent (and therefore superior) faiths.

Obstacles like these do not stand up to scrutiny. Take disparate chronology: No one has any difficulty comprehending that western

Christendom has separate Catholic and Protestant forms although more than fifteen centuries elapsed between the birth of Christ and the day that Martin Luther nailed his 95 theses to the door of the Castle Church in Wittenberg in 1517. A roughly similar time span separates the birth of Christ and Moses' receipt of the Ten Commandments, but that does not impede our use of the term Judeo-Christian. As long as one religious tradition can be seen as growing out of, or being closely akin to, an earlier one, a lapse of time is not a crucial factor.

What about inveterate hatred? Did Muslims fight against Christians and express hatred for them? Yes, from time to time; and their actions and feelings were ardently reciprocated. But did not the early Protestants also pour hatred and scorn on the Catholics and oppose them in incredibly bloody wars? And did not the founders of Protestantism separate themselves from and revile the edifice of Scholastic scholarship that Catholic priests and monks had built up over many generations? By the same token, did not the early Christians scorn the Jews for refusing to recognize their Messiah and declare the vast accumulation of Talmudic legal and moral teachings irrelevant because of the advent of a new law in the person of Jesus Christ? And did not the Jews reciprocate that scorn and condemn those Jews who abandoned the law and became Christians? The sibling linkages between Protestantism and Catholicism and between Christianity and Judaism enshrined in our master narrative of Judeo-Christian civilization depend no more on mutual respect and pacific relations than they do on chronology. Protestants and Catholics may have butchered one another in the past, and Christians may have massacred and vilified Jews and been feared and despised in return, but our appreciation—today—of civilizational kinship among Protestants, Catholics, and Jews is immune to such unfortunate historical memories.

Thus it appears that we do not include Islam in our civilization club mainly because we are heirs to a Christian construction of history that is deliberately exclusive. Western Christendom has regarded Islam as a malevolent Other for many centuries and has invented any number of reasons for holding this view. However, the reasons have come second to the malevolence. Shifting Western portrayals of Islam over the centuries make it clear that reasons for disliking Islam have been constructed as rationales for a preexisting and ongoing animosity and not vice versa. This pattern persists to the present day. Since September 11, 2001 we have read of a Protestant minister's declaration that Muhammad was a demon-possessed pedophile and have heard countless charges that Islam is a religion of terror. These verbal assaults do not draw on previous Islamophobic litanies. Today's anti-Muslim rants are concerned less with recycling Islamophobic canards from centuries past, such as Muhammad being a lying demagogue, than with finding new ways of articulating old hatreds. Under current circumstances, however, the emotional satisfaction some audiences derive from this updating and repackaging of traditional Islamophobia is not worth plunging the world into a series of wars, or nurturing the vilification of a significant portion of the American population.

A fundamental restructuring of Western thinking about relations with Islam calls for a fresh look at history. In the sections that follow, I will outline such a look. The historical development of Western Christendom and Islam parallel each other so closely that the two faith communities can best be thought of as two versions of a common socioreligious system, just as Orthodox Christianity and Western Christendom are considered two versions of the same socioreligious system. For eight centuries, the pathways of development led in the same direction and occasionally virtually overlapped one another.

Latin Christians and Middle Eastern Muslims experienced common challenges in parallel time frames. However, they reacted to these challenges in different ways, and the variations in their responses had consequences in terms of how they responded to the next set of challenges. These divergences accumulated and contributed to a parting of the ways that became evident in the fourteenth through sixteenth centuries. From that time on, Western Christendom, with its overseas colonies, and Islam, now including mass Muslim societies outside the Middle East, followed trajectories that differed markedly, like fraternal twins that are almost indistinguishable in childhood but have distinctive, and not necessarily compatible, personalities as adults. Where in the earlier centuries the sibling traditions moved through their life stages in astonishingly similar ways, after 1500 they began to act as rivals in a worldwide drama. Yet the ways in which they played their roles as rivals still reflected their sibling character and their functioning within a common system: Islamo-Christian civilization.

## Siblings in Step: The Early Centuries

Between 632 and 711, Arab armies carrying Muhammad's revelations from God defeated a broad array of Persian, Byzantine, and Visigothic enemies and seized power over a vast swathe of land stretching from northern Spain to southern Pakistan. From Egypt eastward, the lands that in the seventh century became part of the Caliphate, as historians call the Muslim empire after the title of its ruler, had once been part of Alexander the Great's domain. They had subsequently been heavily influenced by Greek lifestyles and philosophies under Greek, Macedonian, and Persian generals and kings who succeeded to that empire after Alexander's death in 323 B.C.E. West of Egypt, the Caliphate incorporated parts of North Africa, Iberia, and southern France that had formerly belonged to the Roman Empire. There too Roman artists, authors, and political leaders had commonly looked upon Greek culture as a model to emulate. It is fair to say, therefore, that the conquests of the Muslims, inspired by the leadership of their Arabic-speaking prophet, posed the challenge of ruling over, and winning over, a population with a predominantly Greco-Roman cultural orientation in its upper social strata. This is precisely the challenge that the earliest Christians, inspired by the life and death of their Aramaic-speaking messiah, had faced centuries earlier.

The prior experience with Christianity set some of the conditions for later Muslim growth through the circumstance of the largest Christian communities of the age coming abruptly under the control of Muslim rulers. The exact proportion of the total Christian faith community living in Spain, North Africa, Egypt, the Levant (the eastern end of the Mediterranean), the Arabian peninsula, Mesopotamia, and Iran is difficult to estimate; but these lands included three of the four patriarchal centers— Jerusalem, Alexandria, and Antioch—and had produced most of Christendom's leading thinkers and writers, including Jesus and his Twelve Disciples, the Palestinian and Syrian Jews who authored the gospels and epistles of the New Testament, the Egyptian St. Anthony who pioneered the practice of monasticism, the bishops of Alexandria and Antioch who propounded major formulae for understanding the Holy Trinity and the person of Christ, and a series of influential North African theologians culminating in the towering figure of St. Augustine.

To be sure, Anatolia (Turkey) and Greece had large Christian communities and remained unconquered, and Constantinople was a great Christian metropolis and the seat of a patriarch; but being committed to Greek as their ecclesiastical language, and committed to following the eastern patriarchs rather than the Roman popes, these communities played negligible roles in the growth of Latin Christendom, which today we take to represent the historical core of Judeo-Christian or Western civilization. Certain other Christian communities that escaped Muslim conquest, notably the Armenians, Georgians, and Ethiopians, remained even more isolated from subsequent developments in the Latin west.

From the perspective of the core area of later Judeo-Christian or Western Civilization, then, Christianity's seven-century head start over Islam contributed more in terms of accumulated religious thought and institutional experiment, which were equally available to the Muslims through their Christian subjects and Christian converts to Islam, than it did in converting, structuring, and ruling a mass Christian society. Muslims and Latin Christians seeking to extend their faiths in the seventh century were both starting from small territorial and demographic bases. In the year

711, when most of Spain fell to the Muslims, the mass of the western European populace outside Italy and some Christianized areas of France, that is to say, most inhabitants of Germany, Poland, Scandinavia, the British Isles, the Lowlands, and northern France, still revered many gods and followed polytheistic practices, privately if not publicly.

By contrast, believers in polytheism were comparatively rare in caliphal lands. West of Iran, most of the peoples whom the Arabs conquered professed Christianity or Judaism in one form or another. Zoroastrianism, the dominant faith in Iran, did not share the scriptural tradition that Islam claimed kinship with through the Quranic designation of Christians and Jews as "Peoples of the Book," that is, peoples whose religious traditions were based on divine messengers like Abraham, Moses, and Jesus who preceded Muhammad. Peoples of the Book were entitled to retain their religious observances and receive state protection in return for special tax payments and adherence to certain restrictions on social and religious behavior. Nevertheless, Zoroastrianism did resemble Christianity and Judaism in being basically monotheistic, having a well-developed legal and ecclesiastical structure, and transmitting its beliefs and traditions in a canonized sacred text—the Avesta— composed over many centuries. As a practical matter, therefore, the treatment of Zoroastrians by Muslim rulers did not differ substantially from the treatment of Christians and Jews. *De facto* they regarded them as one of the Peoples of the Book rather than as polytheists.

In terms of the centuries-long transformation of religious and social identity that gradually took place within the Caliphate, a process that can be called "Islamization," and the parallel process of "Christianization" that occurred in western and northern Europe, Islam faced a different, and in some ways easier, situation. To win the hearts of the non-Christians of western Europe, Latin Christendom had to accommodate many pre-Christian practices, from Christmas trees to the adoption of certain divinities as Christian saints, while working strenuously to eradicate other beliefs and rituals. Most of the non-Muslims who came under the political sway of the Caliphate, on the other hand, were already oriented toward monotheistic, scriptural religion. Polytheism posed a challenge among the tribal speakers of Berber languages in the highlands and deserts of North Africa and among the nomadic Turks of Central Asia; but in most regions, centuries of Christian, Jewish, and Zoroastrian preaching and community organization had paved the way for a smoother transition to Islam. In this respect, the fact that Muhammad's career followed that of Jesus by six hundred years made it possible for Islam to spread more easily than Latin Christianity. Scriptural monotheists had a much shorter distance to travel, in moral, doctrinal, and organizational terms, to convert to Islam than did European devotees of Wotan, Thor, Jupiter, Epona, Mercury, and a host of other gods whose cults had never developed a comparable scriptural tradition.

Thus these two offshoots of the Judaic scriptural tradition began at roughly the same time to build, through religious conversion, regional societies that would come in time to organize themselves around religious beliefs and practices. The Islamic version of the tradition had the advantage of growing within a region in which many people already knew the tradition well. It also benefited from the continuation of Greek as a learned language, and an established practice of translating Greek texts into Syriac, a Semitic language closely related to Arabic. Though Rome and the western Mediterranean world owed a historical debt to Greek culture, the eclipse there of the Greek language in the waning centuries of the Roman Empire cut Latin Christendom off from much of the pre-Christian Greek heritage. This heritage passed in greater measure to the nascent Muslim society through translations from Greek into Arabic, either directly or by way of intermediate translations into Syriac or Persian.

The process, pace, and indicators of Christian and Muslim conversion vary sufficiently from place to place to make a succinct history difficult. However, over the last few decades, historians of Islam and Christianity, working separately, have tended to discard earlier assumptions of a very rapid pace of conversion. Conquest narratives, both Muslim and Christian, that had once led historians to believe in the instantaneous conversion of battlefield survivors and defeated peoples are now understood to mark at most the commencement of processes of religious penetration that took several, or many, generations. By the same token, the tales of saints and missionaries, more often Christian than Muslim, that attribute prodigies of proselytization to these holy personages are read now less as veracious histories than as exercises in literary piety ornamented by implausibly miraculous events. As for contemporary documents containing concrete data, like lists of bishops attending early Christian councils and locations where coins with Islamic formulae were minted, these seem less convincing than they once did as evidence of religious change among the population at large. A bishop's flock might have numbered only a small percentage of the residents in the territory he presided over, and a mint may indicate nothing more than Muslim governing control at the time and place inscribed on the coins.

In *Conversion to Islam in the Medieval Period*, published in 1979, I argued for a slow chronology of religious change and for a conceptual approach to mass religious change based on models of innovation diffusion originally developed to analyze processes of technological change in the twentieth century. According to this approach, new ideas, whether in the material or the religious realm, depend on the spread of information. No one, it maintains, can adopt something new without hearing about it first. In actual fact, this is not necessarily true. On certain occasions, kings or tribal chiefs became persuaded that conversion to Islam or Christianity would be of benefit and accepted the new faith on behalf of subjects or tribesfolk who had no idea what it meant and may not have been aware that their formal religious identity had changed. However, this sort of nominal conversion, which seems to have been more frequent where polytheistic religious views predominated, whether in Europe, North Africa, or Central Asia, than in the heartland of the already monotheistic Middle East, required generations of follow-up effort to bring about "real" Islamization or Christianization, understood as a deep penetration of scriptural religion into the life styles, world views, and day-to-day piety of a population.

For religious change to have a deep impact on popular beliefs and customs, knowledge of the substance of the religion had to percolate through the countryside and reach into every village and encampment. In societies that were largely illiterate, like those of seventh-century Europe, North Africa, and the Middle East, information spread primarily by word of mouth; and the proponents of the new religious views, whether Christian or Islamic, did not always speak the same language as the people they hoped to bring into the faith. Under these circumstances, significant conversion, that is, conversion that involved some actual understanding of the new religion, as opposed to forced baptism or imposed mouthing of an Arabic profession of faith, must surely have started with fairly small numbers.

Peasants in agricultural villages, the vast majority of the population throughout both conversion regions, may have gone for generations after the defeat of their polytheist chief by a Christian king, or the passage of military control to a conquering Arab army, without access to reliable information about the new faith. In Western Europe, so-called "pagan survivals," beliefs, and practices continuing from pre-Christian times, sometimes in superficially Christian guise, continue to show up for many centuries. In the late sixth century, around the time of Muhammad's birth, Bishop Martin of Braga, a Christian center in northern Portugal that rivaled Toledo for influence in the pre-Muslim Iberian peninsula, deplored local polytheistic practices:

> Observing the Vulcanalia and the kalends, decorating tables, wearing laurels, taking omens from footsteps, putting fruit and wine on the log in the hearth, and bread in the well, what are these but worship of the devil? For women to call upon Minerva when they spin, and to observe the day of Venus at weddings and to call upon her whenever

they go out upon the public highway, what is that but worship of the devil?[9]

Complaints about "pagan survivals" by Muslim writers in the early centuries are comparatively infrequent, though they become more common in later centuries when Islam spreads into south and southeast Asia and sub-Saharan Africa, beyond the region dominated in pre-Islamic times by Christianity, Judaism, and Zoroastrianism. Since the Muslim authorities tolerated sizable Christian, Jewish, and Zoroastrian communities, beliefs and practices particular to those communities not only survived, but eventually stimulated parallel observances among Muslims, most notably pious visitations to shrines revered by one of the earlier faiths and revalidated in Muslim tradition. To this day, for example, the Cave of the Patriarchs in Hebron (Arabic al-Khalil) remains sacred to both Jews and Muslims as the resting place of their ancestors, the various members of the family of Abraham.

One of the themes of modern controversy about Islam in comparison to the West relates to the question of tolerance. Islamophobes have long regarded Islam as unchangingly intolerant because it denies full religious equality to Jews and Christians. The Muslim response has focused on long periods of peaceful and mutually beneficial coexistence during centuries when life in Latin Christendom was blighted by expulsions of Jewish and Muslim minorities and then by warfare between Catholics and Protestants. In fact, Islam and Christianity both proclaimed their hatred and intolerance of polytheism, but until Islam began to expand outside its core area after the year 1000, polytheism seldom posed the problem for Muslim rulers that it posed for European Christians.

The challenge to Latin Christendom was one of eradicating polytheistic belief systems, a process that involved destroying idols and temples, cutting down sacred groves, banning the activities of priests, and prohibiting customary observances. Muslims, meanwhile, worked to persuade adherents of competing, but tolerated, monotheistic faiths to abandon the ways of their ancestors and join the Muslim community. The long-term result was a greater degree of religious homogeneity in Europe than in the Middle East. The Christians effectively eradicated polytheism. But in the process European Christians became comfortable wielding the weapons of religious intolerance: bans, expulsions, inquisitions, excommunications, and charges of heresy. The difference in these matters between the two religions deriving from the Judaic scriptural tradition reflects less a fundamentally different understanding of tolerance than the different preexisting religions in the regions they expanded into.

The innovation diffusion model of conversion indicates a process that worked itself out over a period of several centuries. A comparatively small number of early adopters, probably including an appreciable number of slaves or war captives in both the Christian and Islamic cases, formed a nucleus for expansion that accelerated as their numbers and their ability to communicate with potential converts grew. Language was crucial. The presence of bilingual Jewish communities in many parts of the Roman Empire facilitated the initial spread of Christianity beyond its Aramaic-speaking core. Arabic, however, was spoken only in the Arabian peninsula and the desert borderlands that extended northwards from Arabia between Syria, Jordan, and Iraq. This initial impediment to the spread of knowledge about Islam dissolved only when intermarriage with non-Muslim, non-Arab women, many of them taken captive and distributed as booty during the conquests, produced bilingual offspring. Bilingual preachers of the Christian faith were similarly needed in the Celtic and Germanic language areas of Western Europe.

This slow process of information diffusion, which varied from region to region, made changing demands on religious leaders and institutions. When a faith was professed primarily by a ruler, his army, and his dependents, but was still little known, and even linguistically inaccessible, to the great majority of a region's inhabitants, greatest priority went to servicing the needs of the ruling minority and discrediting, denigrating, or exterminating the practices of the majority. Latin church leaders repeatedly condemned polytheistic practices and celebrated the destruction of cult centers and idols. Muslim leaders limited the public performance of Christian and Jewish rites and the building of new religious buildings, even while guaranteeing freedom of Christian and Jewish belief. Once a few centuries had passed, however, and the new faith had become the religion of the great majority of the population, both Christian and Muslim religious leaders began to occupy themselves with elaborating popular institutions and reaching out to the common people.

In the seventh and eighth centuries, religious leadership in Middle Eastern Islam and Latin Christianity revolved around officials: governors and commanders appointed by the caliphs for the Muslims, bishops installed by popes or regional synods for the Christians. As the respective demographic bases expanded through gradual spread of the faith among the populace, however, so did the number of men desiring to focus their lives on religion. Not everyone could be a bishop or a caliphal governor. From the ninth century onward Latin Christendom and Islam mirrored one another in the rapid growth of bodies of religious specialists. St. Benedict, the founder of Latin monasticism, had lived in Italy in the sixth century, and monasteries dedicated to his rule had arisen in various parts of western Europe. The notion of organizing these monasteries into a Benedictine Order dates to the ninth century, however, as the popularity of monasticism rapidly increased. The parallel phenomenon in Islam involved the rise of the *ulama*, "possessors of religious knowledge," groupings of men in every sizable community who gained popular, that is, nongovernmental, recognition as authorities on Muslim lore and the legal understandings implicit in that lore. Individuals credited with this sort of learning are known as early as the time of Muhammad, but their numbers multiplied throughout the caliphate in the ninth century.

In their similarities and differences these bodies of religious specialists strongly affected the later trajectories of social and political development in their respective areas. One particularly striking similarity was the dedication of each group to a single language of religion—Latin in Europe, Arabic in North Africa and the Middle East—regardless of political or ethnic boundaries. As low levels of literacy hastened the replacement of Latin by the Romance languages and the parallel development of distinctive local dialects of Arabic, uneducated believers had increasing difficulty with the language of the monks and the ulama, a situation that was even more pronounced in regions that spoke entirely different languages, like German and Persian. As a result, religious specialists and/or their writings could move relatively easily from one region to another because they could always find counterparts or audiences who spoke and read Latin or Arabic; but the religious outlook and practice of the uneducated took on a more narrow, local coloration.

The social organization of the monks differed markedly from that of the ulama. Christian monasteries, and convents for women devoted to the religious life, espoused an ideal of prayerful removal from sinful society. Sited initially in rural locales, their personnel took vows of celibacy and seldom traveled. By contrast, in Islam, where from the ninth century on an important goal of religious specialists was collecting the sayings (*hadith*) attributed to the Prophet Muhammad, flight from sin took the form of personal acts of piety, such as night vigils and extensive fasts, rather than removal from society. Travel was encouraged and celibacy uncommon. Where monks pursued important educational and scholarly activities within the monastery, transmitters of hadith, who formed the core of Muslim religious studies at the lower levels, usually lived in cities and taught large numbers of students, many of whom went into trading or craft occupations after finishing eight to twelve years of study. Since the ulama married and had children, families with inherited religious prestige, and the social eminence that went with that prestige, came to play important roles in urban economic and political life by the end of the tenth century. In Europe, men and women from noble families sometimes became monks and nuns, and could wield political influence from those positions; but they seldom established hereditary religious lines.

Closely parallel developments in the area of education eventually lessened this difference in social roles. The deposition of the last Roman emperor in the west in 476 had symbolized a serious decline in literacy, urban life, and economic vitality. Monastic schoolteachers preserved a modicum of learning during the following centuries, but their efforts were little felt beyond their cloistered communities. Across the Mediterranean, the Arab conquest of Syria and Egypt, key provinces of the Byzantine Empire (Eastern Roman Empire), gained for the Caliphate rich lands that had been sheltered from much of the decline experienced in western Europe. The switch from Greek to Arabic as the language of government and the dominant religion, a process that took more than a century, caused discontinuity in traditions of literacy and education; but teaching school and writing books continued at a more rapid pace in the growing Muslim society than in Latin Christendom. Higher learning took place primarily through apprenticeship in government bureaus or among small groups of students gathered around particular masters in mosques or private homes. More formal organization of higher religious studies began with the spread of religious colleges, called *madrasas*, from the eleventh century onward.

These institutions resemble so closely, both in organizational form and scholarly approach, the Christian universities that appeared in major European cities a short time later that some scholars have maintained that there must have been a direct influence of the former on the latter. Be that as it may, it is apparent that both sorts of institution systematically prepared religious specialists for active roles in society. This was no innovation for Islam, where the ulama had always lived active social lives; but for Latin Christendom it reflects the growth in the thirteenth century of fresh ideas about religious roles, represented by the new preaching orders of Dominicans and Franciscans, who dominated university life. The reclusive life of the monk and the nun maintained its attraction, but most university graduates sought active careers giving guidance to the faithful in communities now firmly dedicated to a Christian way of life. Thus the Christian clergy, though still celibate, began to resemble more closely the Muslim ulama as an urban social force.

What distinguished Latin Christendom most fatefully from its Muslim sibling society on the other shores of the Mediterranean Sea was Islam's rejection of a hierarchical ecclesiastical structure. A few ulama served as mosque officials and religious judges, but these positions were not situated within a centralized hierarchy. Christianity had initially grown within the religiously diverse structure of the Roman Empire. Centralized organization had provided strength in the face of competing priesthoods, such as those of Isis and Mithra, and the empire itself had provided an organizational model of provinces and subprovinces. Contrast to this the Caliphate, a conquest state from the death of Muhammad in 632 onward, with no religious hierarchy separate from the political hierarchy of the state. For the first two centuries, state organization assumed that all Muslims were Arabs and therefore sharers in the benefits derived from rule over non-Muslim non-Arabs. Seeing to the economic and political interests of the ruling minority fully occupied the caliphal institutions, leaving spiritual needs, in particular those of a growing number of non-Arab converts, to the informal attention of local groups of pious individuals, the forerunners of the ulama. Yet the Muslim caliphs were well familiar with the ecclesiastical organizations of their non-Muslim subjects. Indeed, they often manipulated the appointment of non-Muslim religious officials. Perhaps this familiarity also made them aware of the bitter struggles for control of the church hierarchy in Eastern Christendom and thus made avoidance of ecclesiastical organization seem virtuous. This is implied by the common Muslim boast that Islam has neither monks nor priests.

In the absence of an ecclesiastical hierarchy, the rapid expansion of the ulama that accompanied the accelerating growth of the Muslim community as a whole in the ninth century took place outside the control of the caliphal government. For a few decades in the middle of the century, a series of caliphs tried to enforce doctrinal discipline on the ulama throughout their realm by requiring allegiance to one particular theological viewpoint. However, the ulama resisted this *mihna*, or "inquisition," some of them to the point of martyrdom, with the result that this belated effort to centralize Islam through a caliphal institution failed. From that time on, groups of local ulama families consolidated social predominance in most cities and from time to time acted politically on behalf of their followers. Yet they never sought to coordinate their activities with ulama groups in other localities. Having given up on doctrinal centralization, the caliphs, along with an assortment of warlords who seized control of one or another province as caliphal authority waned in the tenth century, sometimes patronized locally popular religious figures or doctrines when they thought this might work to their local political advantage. But the ulama never constituted an organized challenge to their rule.

The ulama did succeed, however, in arrogating to themselves the right to elaborate and interpret the religious law. The *sharia*, or Islamic religious law, became increasingly systematic in several variants as the students of major legal theorists took up residence in different cities and popularized their master's teachings. The religious judges appointed (sometimes only nominally) by the rulers from the ranks of the ulama applied that law to everyone—government officials, imams of mosques, and ordinary citizens alike. Nevertheless, large areas of dispute, particularly relating to criminal offenses, they left for civil trial by other government officers.

By contrast, the centralization efforts made by the Catholic Church as the Christian community in western Europe grew in size and diversity over the same time period proved more thoroughgoing. Strong popes, in league with reformers who wanted to improve monastic organization and discipline, asserted the sole and unconditional authority of the church hierarchy. An eleventh-century reform movement based on the monastery of Cluny in France, and owing allegiance solely to the pope, extended centralized control to far-flung daughter monasteries. However, tightening church jurisdiction over priests, monks, nuns, and the properties devoted to their activities, particularly under the forceful reformer Pope Gregory VII (1073–1085), contributed to worsening tensions between rulers and church officials. The canon law of the Catholic Church, which like its Islamic counterpart aspired to be all-embracing, conflicted directly with the legal claims of kings. Though the Catholic Church stood up to the claims of secular rulers more boldly than the ulama did, in the long run, the ulama protected their role as interpreters of the law more effectively. They bent before the undeniable power of the ruler in many instances, but they always insisted on a reaffirmation of the ruler's theoretical subjection to God's commandments. By contrast, the popes collided head-on with powerful Christian rulers in a series of bruising confrontations, and ended up being forced to acquiesce in a steady expansion of royal law.

In sum, the Latin Christian and Muslim reinterpretations of the Judaic religious tradition closely paralleled one another in historical development for some seven centuries after 622. Knowledge of the faith among ordinary people, particularly in the countryside, was slight to nonexistent at the start of the period. Christianity deployed missionaries to spread the word; Islam did not. But Islam had the advantage of spreading in lands that were well prepared to accept the Islamic version of scriptural monotheism. Disregarding regional variations, it is probably not far wrong to assume that developments of the seventh through ninth centuries, among Muslims and Latin Christians alike, lay the foundations of later mass religious expansion at a popular level even as most religious specialists focused their efforts on elaborating doctrine, building their own social and institutional networks, and servicing the needs of ruling elites.

Muslim religious society manifested itself increasingly in cities and their immediate rural hinterlands from the tenth century onward. The same phenomenon occurred slightly later in Latin Christendom where economic recovery from the post-Roman collapse quickened only in the twelfth century. More remote rural locales and fringe regions became religiously oriented still later. In both societies, this later expansion posed a challenge to the religious elites. In responding to that challenge the sibling religious societies set off on diverging paths.

## Same Crisis, Different Responses: The Middle Centuries

Latin Christians tended to look inward during the early centuries. They knew very little about Islam. The orthodox Christians of the east, on the other hand, knew much about Islam and viewed with alarm the loss of Byzantine territory and the steady shrinkage of congregations as the pace of conversion accelerated. Some characterized the confrontation between Christianity and Islam as one of true piety and morality versus the lure of wealth, power, and immoral worldliness, thus prefiguring the exact opposite construction of Muslim-Christian conflict by Islamic ideologues in the twentieth century. The Byzantine emperors, who bore the responsibility for maintaining Christian power in lands bordering the Caliphate, seldom saw eye-to-eye with the popes and kings of Latin Christendom; but they overcame their distaste to urge a joint military enterprise against Muslim rule in the Holy Land. Their cries of alarm helped motivate the crusades, a movement that brought Islam and Latin Christendom into contact, but also heightened the hostility between them.

Between 1095 and 1250, Latin crusaders, with occasional Byzantine help, launched a series of attacks on the Muslim rulers of the Holy Land, initially establishing four small principalities based in the cities of Edessa, Antioch, Jerusalem, and Tripoli at the eastern end of the Mediterranean, the land they knew as Outremer ("Overseas"). Political histories of the crusades usually identify religious fervor and the leaders' desire for land that might be turned into noble estates as the primary Christian motivations. At the economic level, however, Italian trading cities like Pisa, Genoa, and Venice benefited greatly, both from the transportation fees they charged the crusaders and from the growing commerce their merchants carried on with the Muslim lands. While battles and alliances dominate both the historical narratives and the less formal story-telling that the Crusades generated, peacetime activities accounted for most of the cultural contact that took place during that period.

In Spain, where Christian campaigns against Muslim principalities paralleled the Crusades, Christian scholars took advantage of peaceful moments to make Latin translations of Arabic books, which they took back to France and Italy. In Sicily, a Muslim land that was conquered by raiders from northern France during the decades leading up to the Crusades, Arabic and Greek manuscripts also became available for translation. And in the crusader states and adjoining Muslim countries, Italian traders and European nobles who became long-term residents experienced the daily life of Muslim society and brought local customs and ideas back home with them.

During this period, a cornucopia of stimuli from Muslim lands transformed many aspects of European life: philosophy (commentaries on Aristotle), theology (Averroism), mathematics (Arabic numerals), chemistry (gunpowder), medicine (surgical technique), music (lute-playing, troubadour songs), literature (tales that show up in Italian works), manufacturing (glass, paper, woodblock printing), cuisine (pasta, sugar), and the enjoyment of everyday life. The areas most heavily influenced were in southern Europe, but Muslim philosophical views penetrated the universities of northern Europe as well. Muslims today lament the fact that so few people in the West appreciate the massive transfer of culture, science, and technology that began during this period; that transfer, they maintain, paved the way for Europe's later scientific discoveries and intellectual sophistication. This fully warranted lamentation illustrates the power of historical narratives. Where the parallel transmission of ideas and styles from Italy and southern France to northern Europe during the Renaissance is conventionally narrated as an aspect of western

Christian civilization as a whole, few attempts have been made to view Mediterranean cultural developments holistically, either in this period or a few centuries later when Muslim and Jewish refugees from Spain brought "European" ideas southward. It is not the Mediterranean that keeps historians from seeing these flows as happening within a single civilizational complex: Spain and Sicily, where much of the cultural stimulation centered, were parts of Europe. Rather it is the ingrained bias toward viewing anything occurring within Christendom as *entre nous*, and everything emanating from non-Christian sources as contact with the Other.

Comparing the lack of discussion of Muslim cultural influences with Western hyper-awareness of the Crusades themselves, the tendentious reading of Christian-Muslim relations as built on hostility rather than productive relations becomes evident. A parallel might be drawn with today's perceptions of Europe's impact on the non-European (including Muslim) world in the nineteenth century. Postcolonial thinkers from lands subjected to imperialism concentrate on forms of subjection involved with European imperialism that were virtually unperceivable to past generations of traditional European intellectuals. The latter were prone to stress the economic and technical benefits of relations with Europe in the imperialist era, a phenomenon usually described as westernization or modernization, even as they grudgingly acknowledged the oppressive nature of the colonial system. People from formerly colonized societies see these as benefits for which no one is owed any gratitude, given the immensity of the burdens inflicted by the putative imperialist benefactors. In exactly the same manner, the Latin Christians of the twelfth through fourteenth centuries (as well as their descendants today) saw no reason to express gratitude toward, or to recognize the scientific and artistic superiority of, the Muslim societies from whence they were obtaining the ideas, techniques, and industrial processes that would soon catapult Latin Europe along a new and immensely fruitful developmental path. Borrowers have their pride.

The precedence given to violent conflict over cultural borrowing by the dominant historical narratives of this period has obscured parallel developments in the social and religious spheres on the opposite sides of the Mediterranean. Mention has already been made of European universities coming into being in the late twelfth century in a fashion strongly resembling the slightly earlier development of Muslim madrasas. On the Muslim side, these institutions initiated a gradual move toward systematizing preexisting approaches to learning among the ulama. On the Christian side, the universities had a much greater impact because they moved the locus of religious learning out of the cloister and into the town, a phenomenon simultaneously manifested in the proliferation of grand cathedrals and the comparative lessening of investment in abbey (i.e., monastery) churches. Where madrasa professors were simply ulama who were lucky enough to land a tenured position with a salary paid by an endowment, European university professors were usually Dominican and Franciscan friars, members of a type of religious organization that first appeared in the thirteenth century. Friars, like the cathedral canons who came to be organized along similar lines, lived by a set of rules, including celibacy, just as monks and nuns did; but they were not cloistered. They mixed with ordinary citizens, as the ulama always had, and took preaching to the public to be a sacred obligation.

This movement from the cloister into lay society was symptomatic of a need that began to be felt for greater ministration to the religious needs of ordinary people. The deepening of Christian identity at all levels of society, both urban and rural, that became apparent from the twelfth century onward paralleled an identical trend in Muslim society. The pressures that accompanied this climax of the long, slow process of conversion—conversion of minds and souls and not just adoption of a nominal identity—challenged Muslim and Christian religious specialists in similar ways:

- Many lay people wanted to express their religious feelings, and have access to religious knowledge, in their everyday spoken languages instead of in Latin or Arabic.
- People living in the countryside desired closer contact with religious men and women to whom they might look for spiritual guidance,

and they resented the dominance and arrogance of leadership based on monasteries and cathedrals, or on the dryly legalistic presumption of the ulama as sole interpreters of the sharia.

- The growing role of legal matters in religious affairs left many laypersons longing for a more emotional and less legalistic religious experience.
- The penetration of Christianity and Islam into quotidian life led people to seek means of experiencing their faith together in organized groups.

On the Christian side these pressures manifested themselves in two ways, communal living and popular preaching movements. In the twelfth century, women who desired to live a life of religious devotion and charitable work, but who did not wish to join a cloistered order, banded together in communities of Beguines. These town-based societies became popular enough to account, in some instances, for as much as 15 percent of the adult female urban population. The beguines wore plain clothing, worked at crafts, followed strict rules of behavior without necessarily eschewing marriage, and showed a marked inclination toward mysticism. Beguines composed the first European works on mysticism written in vernacular languages, starting with Beatrice of Nazareth's "Seven Manners of Love" written in Flemish in 1233. A parallel movement among men, known as Beghards, included an element of wandering mendicancy. The Church initially blessed the religious commitment of the beguines and beghards but then had second thoughts. Marguerite Porete, who had written a work on mysticism in Old French, was burned at the stake for heresy in 1310. In 1317 the Council of Vienne, after hearing charges of heresy and immorality, abolished beguinage and stipulated that women who wished to live such a life should be brought under strict Church control.

The fate of the beguines and beghards tied into broader fears of heresy that consumed the Church in the thirteenth century. The movement begun by Peter Waldo is representative. A merchant of

Lyons, Waldo gave away his property in 1176 and assumed leadership of a group of men dedicated to a life of holy poverty and bringing the faith to the common people in their own languages. The Pope blessed their way of life but warned them that they could not preach. The Waldenses, as they came to be called, ignored the warning, and their lay preaching brought upon them a charge of heresy. More than eighty Waldenses were burned at the stake in Strasbourg in 1211. Despite suppression, remnants of the Waldenses survived to become Protestants in the sixteenth century.

In fourteenth-century England, John Wyclif, a teacher of theology and philosophy at Oxford, led a somewhat similar movement of "poor priests" who preached to the common people in English. Some of his followers collaborated on translating the Bible into English, the so-called Wyclif Bible. Wyclif was condemned as a heretic, but he escaped burning and died of natural causes in 1384. John Huss in Bohemia did not escape execution. Like Wyclif a well-educated priest, Huss translated Wyclif's writing into Czech and led a militantly anti-Church movement that became involved in wars against Bohemia's Catholic rulers. He was burned in 1415, just over a century before Martin Luther inaugurated the Protestant Reformation in 1517 and turned to translating the Bible into German.

No single movement responded to all of the popular religious pressures that began to become evident in the twelfth century. Some focused on lay people living devout lives, either singly or in groups. Some encouraged mysticism. Some devoted themselves to poverty. Some preached in vernacular languages and translated the Bible into words common people could understand. Some were pacifist. Some were bellicose in the face of Church persecution. All, however, aroused the ire of the Catholic Church and felt the sting of persecution. By the time the definitive break of the Protestant Reformation split Latin Christendom for good in the sixteenth century, mysticism, group living, poverty, and pacifism had necessarily receded. Catholic opposition made militant defense the highest priority.

In Islam, the same pressures gave rise to similar tendencies; but the result over the long term was quite different. The term Sufism is generally associated with these tendencies, but the first manifestations of Sufism in the ninth century differed substantially from what Sufism became in the thirteenth century. Though the word *sufi* probably derives from the patched cloak of wool (Arabic *suf*) that signaled the religious poverty of the wearer, the usual translation of the term is "mystic." This is appropriate for the visionary souls of the early Islamic centuries who yearned for closeness with God and expressed their yearnings in ecstatic, sometimes very poetic, utterances and in acts that their admirers interpreted as miracles. These individuals had many admirers and disciples, and by the eleventh century some of these disciples were living or meeting in houses (variously called *khangah*, *zawiya*, or *ribat*) dedicated to Sufi devotions.

In the thirteenth century these loose assemblies of devotees crystallized into formal brotherhoods (*tariqa*, pl. *turuq*) featuring hierarchical ranks, initiation procedures, set rituals, fixed rules of conduct, and organizational linkages with brotherhoods in other towns dedicated to the rituals of the same Sufi master. Mystic endeavor, increasingly expressed through vernacular poetry, remained the hallmark of the top ranks of these brotherhoods. But many thousands of brothers in the lower ranks, not to mention ordinary citizens who admired the Sufi way of life but were not prepared to make a personal commitment to it, looked upon the brotherhood more as an organization for collective religious experience and moral guidance in everyday life, and as a point of contact with a person of manifest holiness, the leading shaikh of the order.

Sufi codes of conduct frequently stipulated poverty and withdrawal from worldly affairs. Wandering mendicants represented the extreme expression of this. Association with most Sufi orders, however, proved compatible with life in the workaday world, especially for laymen who admired the Sufi life but did not become full members of an order. In this respect Sufism came to represent an integration of religious devotion with a sober and moralistic approach to daily life. The brotherhoods, which acquired phenomenal popularity by the end of the fifteenth century, offered an alternative form of Muslim social and religious experience in which mysticism ultimately played a lesser role than communal devotion to a moral code of behavior sanctified by a saintly figure. Scores of brotherhoods formed, some appealing to higher social ranks and some to lower. The most popular developed geographic networks that spread over thousands of miles irrespective of political divisions.

The ethos of brotherhood Sufism strikingly resembles the ethos of the simultaneous movements within Latin Christendom. Communal devotion, poverty as an expression of detachment from worldly things, mysticism, use of vernacular languages, town-based organization but with penetration into rural areas, and adoption of locally accessible saintly figures as moral models in the place of the increasingly legalistic ulama/clergy are among the specific parallels. The durability of these responses to the popular religious demands that first became evident in this era has lasted to the present day. In Islam, a myriad of popular (and often politically assertive) Muslim organizations pattern themselves consciously or unconsciously on the model of Sufi brotherhoods. Their parallel in Christianity is the contemporary proliferation of new sects, particularly within evangelical Protestantism.

Parallel too was the sense of anger and opposition that the growth of Sufism provoked among the ulama, which resulted on rare occasion in the well-publicized execution of a Sufi shaikh. Though some ulama were themselves Sufis, many others execrated Sufi practices, particularly the dancing and music used in rituals. These opponents of the Sufis would surely have resorted to large-scale persecution if they had had a tradition of identifying and exterminating heretics and an organizational structure suitable for implementing persecution.

In Latin Christendom, the confrontation between established structures and hierarchies and new forms of religious yearning and expression generated increasing friction from 1100 to 1500, with a final culmination in the Protestant Reformation and the shattering of church unity. In Islam, the comparatively weak institutional structure of the ulama could not hold back the new spiritual currents. Where Christendom stood firm and then broke in two, Islam bent and accommodated. By 1500 Sufi orders were well established in most regions. Many ulama remained disenchanted, and the adoption of political militancy by some Sufi orders, most notably in Anatolia (Turkey), provoked wars of suppression; but Sufism was on its way to becoming the primary focus of popular Muslim piety.

The legal impact of the divergent Muslim and Christian responses to new spiritual needs deserves special notice. The shattering of Christian unity culminated in generations of uncommonly vicious warfare between Protestant and Catholic. The competing claims of canon law and royal law over the preceding centuries had set the stage for expressing ecclesiastical disagreements in legal terms. During the Reformation, championing the Catholic or the Protestant cause became an inherent part of royal authority. Preachers and tract writers on both sides inveighed against their enemies and called the faithful to the slaughter. The Peace of Westphalia in 1648 brought the worst of the killing to an end. But by the time the fever had spent itself, a goodly portion of western Europe's population had been consumed, and the remaining scars reinforced a growing conviction that state power must never again be put at the disposal of intolerant religion.

Western secularists today subscribe passionately to the mantra of separating church and state. The logic of their position seems self-evident: religious belief combined with state power is a witch's brew that poisons all who consume it. It happened that way in European history. The lesson was learned. From Westphalia on, royal will would take precedence over the dictates of popes and preachers. Individual kings might still be fanatics, but in the interests of the crown, their successors might choose to marry or form alliances across religious boundaries.

But this break between church and state didn't happen in Islam. Sufi devotion could occasionally mobilize armies. One such army powered the Safavid family to dominion over Iran in 1501. And a will to extirpate Sufi heterodoxy could occasionally prompt rulers to launch military campaigns. In Ottoman Turkey it happened several times between 1300 and 1500. But by and large, the Sufi brotherhoods that became the paramount expressions of mass piety after 1400 lived in harmony with one another and cooperated with state officialdom. Rulers were more likely to patronize eminent living Sufis and arrange to be buried at the feet of deceased saints than they were to charge them with heresy or disloyalty. Where being a Catholic or a Protestant implicitly charged Christian monarchs with responsibilities to defend their faith against the other persuasion, in Islam the communal prayers of the mosque, the proceedings of the courts of religious law, and the Sufi rituals of devotion fit comfortably together in the lives and worldviews of most Muslim rulers. Islamic law, in the abstract, remained universal and unchallenged while the canon law of the Catholic Church receded in the face of post-Westphalian royal writ, and the Protestants never produced an all-encompassing legal philosophy of their own.

## The Siblings Part: The Later Centuries

While Islam and Christendom remained locked in hostile sibling embrace after 1500, accidents of history carried their competition into new arenas. Between 1200 and 1400 a series of Mongol and Turkic assaults exposed the Muslim Middle East to new influences from Central Asia and China while between 1400 and 1500 a series of maritime discoveries opened European eyes to exotic new worlds in Africa, Asia, and the Western Hemisphere. These parallel experiences shaped the respective economic and political futures of western Christendom and Middle Eastern Islam. Later Muslim dynasts struggled for centuries to re-create the great and prosperous Eurasian land empire of Genghis Khan, while the Europeans—except for the Russians, who too had experienced Mongol rule—became fixated on maritime empire.

With respect to religion, the sibling faiths faced parallel challenges. The two centuries preceding the onslaught of the Mongols in 1218 had seen substantial Muslim expansion into India and sub-Saharan Africa. Since the cultural traditions of these new regions were not based on the Hellenistic worldview that had permeated the Mediterranean lands in the centuries following the conquests of Alexander the Great, the challenge of absorbing the new territories into an Islamic realm differed greatly from the one facing the Arab conquerors of the first Islamic century. Muslim rulers confronted populations they deemed idolatrous and responded with a fluctuating mix of military action, persecution, commercial exploitation, and religious preaching, the latter conducted mostly informally by the newly emerging Sufi brotherhoods. The experience of Mongol empire accelerated these tendencies by inspiring post-Mongol shahs and sultans to grab more and more territory.

Western Christianity experienced a parallel confrontation with what it considered idolatry in enclaves along the African coast and, more extensively, in the New World. Like the shahs and sultans, Europe's monarchs responded with a mix of military action, persecution, commercial exploitation, and vigorous preaching, mostly conducted in highly organized fashion by Dominicans, Franciscans, and Jesuits acting explicitly at royal command.

Taking Islam and Christianity together, scriptural monotheism in the Semitic tradition seemed to be on the march everywhere. But looking broadly at the period 1500 to 1900, western Christendom and Middle Eastern Islam exhibit proselytizing dissimilarities. It is a commonplace of modern Euro-American historical thinking that Europe surged ahead during these centuries and left the Muslim world in the dust. Words like "decline," "stagnation," and "backwardness" are hurtful to Muslim ears in view of Islam's earlier centuries of glory; but the contrast in wealth and material power that had so much favored the Muslims before the sixteenth century undeniably grew to favor the western Christians.

But wait. Perhaps there is another way of looking at things. Suppose instead of inquiring about imperial riches, one were to ask what percentage of the world Muslim community today is composed of the descendants of people who converted to Islam between 1500 and 1900. The answer would surely exceed 50 percent: pretty much all of Bangladesh, Malaysia, and Indonesia; enormous groups of sub-Saharan Africans; most of the Muslims of Pakistan, India, and China; substantial populations in southeastern Europe and Central Asia. By contrast, if one were to ask what percentage of today's Roman Catholic and Protestant populations descend from ancestors who converted to Christianity between 1500 and 1900, the answer would be well under 20 percent, and would fall to a very low level indeed if one excluded the Americas, Australia, the Pacific islands, and the southern one-third of Africa—lands where the European Christians encountered no religion of competitive sophistication. In the great Afro-Eurasian land bloc and the adjoining region of southeast Asia, European Christianity and Islam went head to head in a contest for the souls of the indigenous peoples, and Islam unquestionably won.

If today one were to measure the long-term success of competing socioreligious systems, therefore, according to their demonstrated appeal over recent centuries, one would be forced to conclude that Islam pushed decisively ahead between 1500 and 1900 while, after an initial surge, European Christianity eventually declined, stagnated, and fell backward. Of course, no one measures success in this fashion—except for contemporary Muslim ideologues who relentlessly expose Europe's lack of religiosity and morality and encourage their Muslim audiences to hold firm to the right ways of their tradition. But obviously this was not always the case.

From the dawn of Christianity down to the nineteenth century—and still today in evangelical Christian circles—the winning of souls took precedence over wealth and power as a sign of success. Our master narratives of European history still put great emphasis on the triumphant spread of Christianity until roughly the nineteenth century, when missionary efforts to extend the faith are increasingly portrayed as quirky, if not downright distasteful.

An uncharitable observer might opine that European Christians happily equated the spread of their faith with the spread of civilization right down to the point when it became evident that their faith was no longer spreading very effectively, and then switched to a different set of civilizational indices: miles of railroad track, factory output, military might, size of empire, etc. Of course, the fact that Islam surged ahead conversion-wise as Christianity stagnated did not play a role in this switch of evaluative indices. Christians, after all, tended to regard Islam as a form of barbarism and usually alleged that its success derived from theological shallowness and pandering to polytheism. But Islam's proselytizing surge during its centuries of so-called "decline," and Christianity's proselytizing stagnation, cannot seriously be questioned. Nor can it be denied that the aggregate success of Islam and Christianity in becoming the world's dominant religion(s) over the past five centuries is as striking a historical phenomenon as the worldwide triumph of European imperialism.

The counterargument can be made that the two experiences of religious expansion do not bear comparison because the European Christians, unlike the Muslims, were spectacularly open to new ideas and in the process of achieving, in the Enlightenment, a transcendent, post-scriptural understanding of the world that many Muslims are still reluctant to embrace. But this historical construction, too, is open to query. Were Muslim societies truly closed to new ideas? In a word, no. The world Muslim community during these centuries embraced scores of new populations in Africa and Asia, learned their languages and customs, found common ground with their traditional institutions and arts, and showed the same remarkable adaptability that had marked the initial spread of Islam in the seventh and eighth centuries and later the growth of the Sufi brotherhoods in the middle centuries. By contrast, the Europeans eagerly collected plants, animals, and artifacts from exotic lands, and made very good use of some of them. But they were not nearly so open to learning exotic languages, assimilating local customs, and respecting traditional social and artistic values. The new ideas that the Europeans were open to were their own, not those of their imperial subjects. When Europe was comparatively weak in the middle centuries, cultural borrowing from Muslim neighbors made good sense. But with empire came a conviction of superiority that closed most western minds. Western Christendom offered nothing, for example, to compare with the annual pilgrimage to Mecca as a place where believers from every land, and speaking every language, could sojourn and learn from one another in conditions of racial and spiritual equality.

So the siblings that had for so long trodden the same developmental path parted company. European monarchs trumpeted their intent to Christianize the world, but settled for economic and military might. Muslim rulers in the Middle East, North Africa, and India (Morocco, sub-Saharan Africa, and Southeast Asia followed different trajectories) strove mightily to create rich and powerful land empires, but only sporadically thought of converting their subject peoples to Islam. Would it be oversimplifying matters to say that when scriptural monotheism enjoyed the political and financial backing of powerful rulers, efforts at proselytization eventually faltered; but when the job of spreading the faith fell to unofficial Sufi merchants and wayfarers acting beyond the reach of Muslim rulers, Islam succeeded? What this formula leaves out is a dynamic that in some parts of Africa and Asia saw "unofficial" Islam succeed precisely because it was a potent alternative to the Christianity being propounded by the imperialists. If imperialism was a form of foreign tyranny, Islam, unwavering in its vision of a universal legal and moral order, increasingly became the bastion of resistance to tyranny.

According to the "clash of civilizations" hypothesis, the (Judeo-Christian) West has always been and always will be at odds with Islam. According to the Islamo-Christian civilization model, Islam and the West are historical twins whose resemblance did not cease when their paths parted. The best way to substantiate the latter contention is to ask whether the various Western and Islamic societies of today are truly different. As most specialists acknowledge, a significant portion (approximately 12 to 15 percent) of Muslims in many countries would like to see Islamic governments impose and enforce a moral and behavioral order that they see as an integral part of being Muslim. Another percentage, seemingly of about the same magnitude, or perhaps a bit smaller, would like to live in an essentially secular society and conduct their spiritual lives through private observances. These two minorities are generally scornful of one another and contest for the allegiance of the less ideological majority. By comparison, in the United States, the country that Muslim ideologues see as standing for the whole of Western society, a significant minority, made up of conservative Christians from the heartland, publicly pressures the government to impose its religiously-based moral standards on the country as a whole. Another minority, the battered, bicoastal remnants of American liberalism, sees itself as holding true to rights and freedoms that are guaranteed in the Constitution but threatened by the "Religious Right." The two minorities scorn one another and contest for the allegiance of the residual majority.

True to the ongoing sibling relationship of the two societies, American commentators on Islam characterize militant Muslims as the dominant voice in the Islamic world, and scarcely recognize the presence there of liberal minds. At the same time, they characterize the American "Religious Right" as something completely different: either a moral force for good, if they belong to that camp, or an aberrant and anti-democratic phenomenon that cannot be readily explained. Muslim commentators, on the other hand, whether militant or secular, see America as a secular land of sin, salesmanship, and superficiality and seem totally unaware of the admirable qualities that most Americans exhibit in their daily life. Neither religious nor secular Muslims have much use for the American "Religious Right," particularly in view of its current romance with Zionism. As for their own societies, liberal Muslims deplore religious militancy and wish for it to go away while militant Muslims see homegrown liberals as agents of American influence or abettors of dictatorship. Neither sibling seems capable of seeing itself or its twin in a comprehensive and balanced fashion, because neither is prepared to recognize itself in the mirror.

Looked at as a whole, and in historical perspective, the Islamo-Christian world has much more binding it together than forcing it apart. *The past and future of the West cannot be fully comprehended without appreciation of the twinned relationship it has had with Islam over some fourteen centuries. The same is true of the Islamic world.* The case for Islamo-Christian civilization as an organizing principle of contemporary thought is rooted in the historical reality of those centuries. One might hope that historians of Western Civilization and of Islam will see the value of readjusting their perspectives to take this reality into account. But our society cannot wait for the sluggish current of historiographical reflection to carve a new channel. The case for Islamo-Christian civilization rests more immediately on the need of all Americans to find common ground with our Muslim diaspora communities at a time when suspicion, fear, draconian government action, and demagoguery increasingly threaten to divide us. Islamo-Christian civilization is a concept we desperately need if we are to have any hope of turning an infamous day of tragedy into a historic moment of social and religious inclusion.

*Theory predicted that rulers freed from the bonds of the sharia would seek absolute power, and they regularly lived up to that expectation.*

CHAPTER 2

# What Went On?

THE QUESTION "What went wrong?" has emerged as a compelling starting point for discussions of the contemporary Middle East. It appears to be a reasonable historical question. Even within the Arab and Muslim world there is broad recognition of weakness and failure, and widespread fear that the passage of time only makes matters worse. It is important to ask the right questions, but one cannot do so until one has explained why the question that is currently being asked doesn't work.

"What went wrong?" stands history on its head. The notion that something went wrong presumes a comparative perspective in which there is a clear notion of how things should have gone, something against which the actuality of failure can be measured. One might hypothesize an example from the Civil War. The leadership of the Confederate States of America sought victory; they lost. In the aftermath, their asking "What went wrong?" would have made good historical sense. It was their plans, after all, that had failed; and the question would have presumed this perspective.

But whose perspective is involved when the question is raised for the Middle East? Bernard Lewis, the popularizer of the phrase, puts it this way at the outset of his book *What Went Wrong?*:

> What went wrong? For a long time people in the Islamic world, especially but not exclusively in the Middle East, have been asking this question. The content and formulation of the question, provoked primarily by their encounter with the West, vary greatly according to the circumstances, the extent, and duration of that encounter and the events that first made them conscious, by comparison, that all was not well in their own society.[1]

This introduction avoids telling us just who in the Islamic world has been asking the question; but it does make it clear that the question is comparative in intent. Why do people in the Islamic world live in circumstances they consider to be so much worse than those of people in the West? As he proceeds with the book, Lewis details the terms of this comparison. The Islamic world, and especially the Middle East, sadly trails the West in freedom, gender equality, secularism, economic and intellectual vitality, material living standards—in fact, in just about everything.

But what path should have been taken? What caused the Muslim societies to veer from that path? Comparison alone sheds no light. Comparatively speaking, the United States lagged far behind Europe in music, drama, and the visual arts well into the twentieth century. This was recognized on both sides of the Atlantic. But no one would begin an analysis of this disparity by asking "What went wrong?" because social and cultural circumstances in the two regions were so disparate that there is no reason to suppose that they should have attained equal levels of achievement.

The Muslim world never possessed a road map with a clearly marked path leading to a promised land of equality with Europe. To be sure, some rulers and statesmen sought to be as rich as the

European powers, or as powerful militarily, and a few believed that liberal principles and governmental institutions might help them toward those goals. No one, however, dreamt that an adroit deployment of European ideas and techniques would lead, by the end of the twentieth century, to societies, governments, and economies that would be as free, as prosperous, and as dominant as those of Europe and North America. The reason I can say this with confidence is that no one in Europe and North America knew where the ship they were sailing on was heading. The great goals that the West now believes it has achieved—equality of race and gender, peace and unity among European nations, global dominance by Euro-American economic enterprise unencumbered by the artificial boundaries and rivalries of empire, and the unquestioned dominance of democratic government—were invisible to Europeans and Americans alike throughout the whole of the nineteenth century and most of the twentieth.

It is comforting to think, when things are going well, that where you are is where you were destined to be, that you took the right path. Ever since the Nazis were defeated, the Soviet Union collapsed, the war-weary European empires gave up their colonies, and France and Switzerland finally gave women the vote, it has been tempting to believe that this is how history was meant to come out. Yet things almost went horribly and irrecoverably bad, as scores of millions of graves marking the victims of European war, holocaust, and oppression testify.

To the extent that observers in the Muslim world tried from time to time to look at things in a comparative perspective, and to visualize ways of countering or matching the incontestable and growing economic and political superiority of Europe, their standard of comparison was not late-twentieth-century Euro-American society. It was the dominant European society or political regimes of their own day, the imperialists, the fascists, and the communists, as well as the liberal-minded democrats.

In 1810, when Muhammad Ali was dreaming of making Egypt as strong as any European power, his standard of comparison was

Napoleon: no democracy, no liberal values, just the massive power of the imperial military state and the will of an absolute monarch. Such was the path he chose. In 1856, in the aftermath of the Crimean War, when an Ottoman sultan issued a series of decrees instituting reforms along European lines, his standard of comparison was the France of Napoleon III and the Great Britain of Queen Victoria: no gender equality, no international economic synergy, no universal education, just the velvet glove concealing the imperialist fist. Such was the path taken two decades later by Sultan Abdülhamit II. When Mustafa Kemal Atatürk was laying down the principles of the Turkish Republic in the 1920s, his standards of comparison were Benito Mussolini and Josef Stalin: no political openness, no freedom of expression, no economic liberalism. He took the same path.

The marvel of Europe at the outset of the twenty-first century is that despite the horrors of the preceding two centuries, it has said goodbye to empire, set aside national rivalries and military confrontation, made a universal commitment to democracy and civil liberties, and recognized, at long last, the fundamental equality of all human beings. It is a wonderful outcome, but not one that was predictable or inevitable, much less the consequence of a developmental path that could have been observed and followed to a similar end by people in other lands. The idea that people in the Middle East once embraced the goal of becoming like Europe and hoped that by adopting European ideas and institutions they would someday experience all of the liberal values we recognize in the Europe of today is nonsense. It assumes a historical outcome for Europe itself that no one even in Europe could have predicted.

So where did the idea that something "went wrong" come from? Since Bernard Lewis popularized the notion, his first important scholarly work, *The Emergence of Modern Turkey*, is a reasonable place to look. He completed the book in 1960, but its genesis dates to 1949–50 when he went to Turkey to pursue research. He relates his feelings about the Turkey of 1950 in the preface to the book's third edition, published in 2002, the year *What Went Wrong?* also went to press:

> Several factors, it seems in retrospect, determined the basic approach, the dominant conception, and the final conclusions of the book . . . In my historical studies, I began with medieval Islam, proceeded to the Ottoman Empire, and then, later, to modern Turkey. . . . The fact that I first came to Turkey, so to speak, from the past and from the south [i.e., the heartland of medieval Islamic civilization, Lewis' first area of research] instead of from the present and from the west, gave me a different—and I would claim better—understanding of the country, of its history and culture, and therefore of its problems.[2]

I too spent many years immersed solely in medieval Islamic studies before turning my attention on the modern Middle East, and I share Lewis' self-serving opinion that coming at the modern period from the medieval Islamic past has given me a different—and indeed better—understanding of the region's history, culture, and problems. Lewis again:

> A second determining factor, of at least equal importance, was the world situation during my formative years and during the period when the book was begun and completed. For the men and women of that generation, their whole lives, their every thought, was dominated and indeed shaped by the titanic struggles in which they had participated, or which they had at the very least witnessed—the defeat and, so it seemed at the time, the destruction of fascism by an alliance of democrats and communists; the ensuing struggle, commonly known as the Cold War, between these former allies to decide which of them would shape the future of the world; the emergence of a third, neutralist bloc in some of the countries liberated by the withdrawal of the western Empires. In the fifties, these issues loomed very large, and the choices before us still retained something of the clarity, even the starkness, which they had through the war years and which they have subsequently lost.[3]

By "the men and women of that generation" it is clear that Lewis is referring primarily to Europeans and Americans. For the Palestinians displaced by the Israeli triumph of 1948, the Egyptians who rose as a nation to support Gamal Abdel Nasser after the revolution of 1952, the Iranians who cried in anguish when the CIA and British intelligence helped the Shah crush Mohammed Mossadegh's nationalist movement in 1953, and the Algerians who initiated a war to free their country of French colonial rule in 1956, "their whole lives, their every thought, was dominated and indeed shaped" by their own national dramas, not by the defeat of fascism and the struggle against communism. And it is difficult to recognize the thrill of achieving national independence, or the torment of falling short of that goal, in what Lewis blandly recalls as the "emergence of a third, neutralist bloc in some of the countries liberated by the withdrawal of the western Empires." The issues of the fifties that gripped the western men and women of Lewis' generation were decidedly not the issues that gripped the same generation of men and women in the Muslim world.

From Lewis' standpoint, however, the startling political spectacle of 1950 was understandably exhilarating. In free elections, Turkey's newly founded Democrat Party, led by Adnan Menderes, unseated the Republican People's Party that had dominated every Turkish government since the establishment of both republic and party by Atatürk himself. The military overthrow of Menderes, and his trial and execution for violating the constitution, were still ten years in the future. And with the clouds of the Cold War gathering, no one was yet ready to speculate that Turkey's sudden turn toward democracy had something to do with American financial and military support extended under the Truman Doctrine, or with a desire, realized two years later, to be accepted into NATO. (As today Turkey confronts explicit European demands for liberalizing reforms as conditions for acceptance into the European Union, the notion that history is repeating itself is hard to resist.)

This clarity of choice gave a special significance to the already dramatic development of events in Turkey at the time when this book was conceived and written. What could be more illuminating, more in accord with the mood of optimism that victory had brought and which the Cold War had not yet dissipated, than the spectacle of a nation liberating itself from ancient bonds—a country of age-old authoritarian habits and traditions turning to democracy; a regime [i.e., the Republican People's Party] that had for decades enjoyed a virtual monopoly of power setting to work, systematically, to prepare, organize, and preside over its own electoral defeat. Even now, more than fifty years later, despite all the ensuing setbacks and frustrations—and there have been many—no one who was there at the time can ever forget the excitement, the exhilaration, of Turkey's first giant step towards a free and open society.[4]

I would not dream of disputing what Lewis says of the exhilaration of the moment, or of its continuing force fifty years later. "The mood of optimism that victory had brought" is another question. Whose victory? Whose optimism? Turkey was neutral during World War II; Iran was militarily occupied and its ruler deposed; the rest of the Middle East lived under more or less oppressive imperialist control. Political aspirants in Egypt, Palestine, Iraq, and Iran, to name but four, had tentatively reached out to the Axis powers for support against imperialism. Six months after VE day, Britain and France had announced no plans for loosening their imperial grip on Muslim lands, nor had the Soviet Union shown any indication of adhering to a wartime commitment to evacuate Iranian territory. In the absence of specific corroborating information, therefore, it would seem that to the extent that the mood of optimism that Lewis describes was shared by the Turks, it was not for the same reasons.

The question of who has been asking "What went wrong?" thus finds its answer. It is not unnamed "people in the Islamic world," but rather Lewis himself. He witnessed in 1950, with decidedly European eyes, what he took to be "Turkey's first giant step towards a free and open society," and the vision is undiminished more than fifty years later. Is there a free and open society in Turkey today? No. Is there a free and open society anywhere in the

Muslim Middle East, or in the Muslim world at large? No. What went wrong? Lewis' vision of a goal provides the comparative standard. Lewis' perception of a derailment on the way to that goal motivates the question.

Were it not for the publicity given to his question, there would be no reason to address it in such detail. Every westerner who visits the Middle East, whether only an occasional visitor or one who lives there for a longer period, encapsulated in the typical cocoon of an expatriate community, generalizes too grandly from his or her experiences. (The same holds true for Middle Easterners who sojourn in Europe and America.) Someone who happened to go to Iran for the first time in 1971 during the build-up to the Shah's celebration of 2,500 years of Iranian imperial greatness might understandably have come away with a vision of enduring autocratic grandeur, just as someone who went for the first time in 1979 might understandably have come home convinced that Islamic revolution was the wave of the future. Like Lewis, the former might subsequently have wondered what went wrong when the Shah abandoned his throne to Ayatollah Khomeini, and the latter might have wondered what went wrong when the overwhelming electoral victory of President Khatami led to harsh repression of dissent rather than liberalization. Visitors collect snapshots and connect dots. They examine scattered samplings of trees and extrapolate forests. When they ask what went wrong, their standard of comparison is of their own making.

What, then, do people within the Muslim world ask? Which of the many constructions of history most helps to explain the well-documented miseries of today? The list of explanations is long: absence of political freedom; squandering of national wealth on armaments; suppression of dissent and free expression; stagnant economic development; export of capital by people of wealth; massive unemployment; stultifying educational institutions; religious, ethnic, and gender inequality and discontent; excessive population growth; etc. Certain constructions command great attention. For many, what has seemed most important is the creation of the state of Israel, and the support of Israel by the United States from 1967 on. For others, the heavy legacy of imperialism, in all of its many forms, tells the tale best. Still others focus on western conspiratorial plots to strip Muslims of their capacity to act effectively in their own interests. And a few, like Lewis, find the dead hand of Islam behind every failure. What these constructions hold in common is the notion of a villain, a malevolent force persistently preventing good things from happening.

Refuting these multifarious readings of history would be of little value. Those who hold them dear are unlikely to relinquish them, and most of them make some degree of sense. In any case, there is no need for a single unitary explanation of so far-reaching a phenomenon as the desolation besetting the Muslim world. Instead of refutation, I would propose a question that is too seldom considered: What went right?

## What Went Right?

Lewis quite reasonably asks us to consider the viewpoints of people in the Islamic world as they considered various disparities between their own situations and those of citizens in western countries. Some of these viewpoints are contained in memoirs, travel accounts, political tracts, and novels. Others can be read into the undertakings of rulers from the early nineteenth century to the present, from Egypt's Muhammad Ali and the Ottoman sultan Mahmud II to the likes of Husni Mubarak and the recently enthroned dynastic rulers of Morocco, Jordan, Syria, Bahrain, and Qatar.

All of these individuals, and thousands of others whose names have gone unrecorded, have observed significant differences between their own societies and those of Europe. But they have not all observed the same differences. One writer will comment on female shoulders fetchingly bared by French ball gowns, another on European scientific achievements, a third on the shocking and awesome firepower of western armies. As for the rulers, they typically recognize disparities in economic and military power but disagree in appraising the source of these disparities. Some want less Islam, some want more. Some want freer trade; some want a closed door.

Nor do Arab and Muslim observations always reflect a sense that things are better in the West. The Muslim zealot Sayyid Qutb, the martyred firebrand of today's revolutionary wildfire, spent the years 1948–1950 in the United States, observed a multitude of differences, and concluded that Islam afforded a better path to the future. So it is far from self-evident that comparative observation results in a consistent sense of what the Muslim world is lacking, or even in a sense that differences with the West must always be understood as Muslim deficiencies. Moreover, when differences are cast as deficiencies, the nature of the deficiency, and the recommendations for rectifying it, differ from observer to observer.

To start at the level of the individual, one example will suffice. Writing from the most mundane and practical standpoint in the 1890s, a little-known Egyptian official named Yusuf Bushtali focused on day-to-day life in his *Hidyat al-Muluk fi Adab al-Suluk* ("The Conduct of Kings on the Propriety of Behavior"), subtitled in French *Etiquette*.[5] He takes as his topic "the entry of western civilization and the customs of its people in our eastern land; the acceptance by easterners of the acquisition of the westerners' sciences and arts; and the imitation of them in matters of eating, drinking, residential living, and dressing."[6]

The westerners, he observes, "spend dirhams and dinars and cross seas and deserts to come to this land in order to study our customs. They observe our homes, our mosques, and our meeting places. They attend our weddings, our festivals, our birthdays, and our funerals. Then they write fat volumes about them. They buy our goods and the crafts of the people of our country for the highest prices, and they use them to ornament their homes, their museums, and the palaces of their rulers. They study our languages and investigate the traces of our forefathers. They decipher the secrets our ancestors have written on the faces of hard stones in order to understand their customs and knowledge."

Then, after enumerating and praising the traditional and continuing virtues of his countrymen, he declares: "It is perfectly clear that studying the customs and peoples of the West is an absolute obligation"—here he uses *fard wajib*, a technical phrase from Islamic law—"on every easterner who wants to mingle with them and draw close to them in order to live among them as an acknowledged equal, not as someone who is below them in understanding and elementary education."[7]

Four hundred pages of minutely observed description of western customs follow. The topics range wide: riding in a carriage, calling cards, party games, etiquette at dinner, wedding gifts, dances, and a long section on western foods, including lists of dishes in French, English, and Arabic with line engravings showing how to carve a chicken or a rabbit.

Who was Bushtali? Nobody. A minor government official. The histories of modern Arabic literature ignore him, and his prescription of slavish imitation of western ways offends the Arab nationalist sensibilities that surfaced two decades after his writing and continue today. But his approach to the problem of difference shows considerable insight of a behaviorist kind. The differences he sees between the Egyptians and the Europeans are clearly deficiencies. Though he puts the burden of learning how to behave like the westerners only on those Egyptians who want to mingle with them, he explicitly states that the cost of not doing so is European disdain. Furthermore, Egyptians studying the behavior of westerners are not mirroring the practices of westerners examining the behavior, languages, etc. of Egyptians. European ethnography, archaeology, and orientalism yield fat volumes, but he never says that the Europeans aspire to be treated as equals by the Egyptians. His prescription for his countrymen aims not at producing ethnographic tomes, though that is precisely what he himself is doing, but at producing equality of status, something that involves not only social acceptance, but also acknowledgement of a parallel level of understanding. An Egyptian who behaves exactly like a westerner, he believes, will be received as a westerner.

One may wonder whether Bushtali actually believed that reading a manual on etiquette would help very much. Nevertheless, his basic perception was both sound, and very widespread. Untold thousands of Muslims consciously or unconsciously acted on the syllogism Bushtali sets forth: A) Europeans do not respect or accept as equals non-Europeans who behave in "native" fashion. B) Europeans *do* grant acceptance to non-Europeans who learn to dress, converse, and otherwise comport themselves in a European manner. C) Therefore, non-Europeans who wish to be accepted as equals must learn to comport themselves in European fashion. This simple idea, whether consciously articulated or intuitively sensed, continues the guide the lives of many Arabs and Muslims down to the present day.

Ingrained stereotypes relating to the Arab and Muslim world over the past century or so contain many examples of westerners reacting favorably to "natives" fitted out with European clothes, manners, and social graces, and other examples of non-Europeans being disparaged for trying unsuccessfully to ape western customs. These reactions have lately reinforced political sentiments in the warmth accorded impeccably tailored Arabs like Jordan's late King Husain or Saudi Arabia's ambassador to the United States, Prince Bandar bin Sultan, as compared with the caustic comments often made about Yasir Arafat's unshaven face and inappropriate military garb. But what alternative is there for someone who wants western respect? Nonwesterners who stick to their own costumes and practices may sometimes be admired as colorful denizens of semi-civilized lands. Afghanistan's Hamid Karzai with his colorful robe and Afghan hat comes to mind. Derisive cartoons of Arab oil sheikhs in gowns and checkered headdresses, however, associate the retention of nonwestern styles and habits with primitive, if not vicious, inclinations. As for Europeans who "go native" and adopt local dress and customs—a not uncommon affectation among nineteenth-century Englishmen—they are regularly dismissed as eccentrics or mountebanks. A Turk or Arab or Persian wearing a business suit may well be treated as an equal. An American, Englishman, or German wearing a turban is a fool. As Bushtali saw so clearly, cultural exchange between west and nonwest presumes western superiority.

Were Bushtali alive today, he would surely remark that things have obviously gone right for many Arabs and Muslims. Kuwaiti businessmen with flats in London, first-class tailors, and degrees from American and British universities are unquestionably received as equals, and their opinions accorded respect, in the western circles they frequent. Iranian and Lebanese doctors practicing in the United States stand at the highest levels of their profession. Elegantly attired Palestinian professors at renowned universities write cutting-edge works that command worldwide respect. In Bushtali's day, such a prospect was almost unthinkable, and it is still hard to imagine it happening if the individuals in question had chosen to rely on their personal talents alone without the accompaniment of a western wardrobe, education, and comportment.

Needless to say, access to these desiderata of western acceptance is not, and never has been, available to everyone. Ironically, those individuals who by virtue of family position, wealth, or espousal of non-Muslim religious beliefs have had the greatest opportunities for assimilation to western modes of thought and behavior are often the ones who feel most acutely the disparity between the life circumstances of their compatriots and those of native-born Europeans and Americans. Their anguish testifies to the fact that while assimilation may enable individuals to bridge the gulf in life circumstances, the problems of their home societies have to be addressed in a systemic fashion.

Has the failure to keep pace with the west been rooted, then, in wrong-headed leadership? In the history of nonwestern nations trying to close the gap with Europe, the universally recognized paragon of leadership is the Meiji emperor in Japan. Between 1868 and his death in 1912, Meiji presided over a transition in almost every facet of Japanese life. A constitution and parliamentary electoral system came into being. Equality of status was achieved in international treaties. Industrial growth and military reforms led to victory in the Russo-Japanese War of 1905 and subsequent recognition as a great power. Whatever the problems besetting the Japanese economy today, no one, either Japanese or western, finds serious fault with the path taken during the Meiji period.

Meiji himself, however, was not the one who charted that path. He chose the people to put in authority, and he stood behind their decisions; but he did not govern and did not promote his own personal ideas. His surviving writings consist almost exclusively of poems. Though he observed military maneuvers, and insisted on sharing the personal discomfort of his soldiers, he did so because he thought it was his duty rather than because he wanted to learn about strategy or join in war planning. He donated money to victims of disaster, but his reluctance to spend money on himself kept him from building a suitable palace in his capital city. Very well read in the classics of Confucian thought, he served his nation with humanity and diligence and was deeply mourned on his passing.

By comparison, the leaders of the Arab and Muslim world who have most ardently sought equality with the West have also been consumed with dreams of unlimited personal power. As heads of state they have shared a common set of goals: to prolong or achieve independence from European control, to make their countries militarily and economically stronger, to tighten controls over their domestic populations, to develop and make more European the skills of those who serve their governments, and to free themselves from real or potential criticism by Muslim men of religion.

Yet maximizing personal power has always loomed as an unspoken end surpassing all of these proclaimed goals. Muhammad Ali, a military commander sent by the Ottoman sultan to Egypt to help regain control after the withdrawal of Napoleon's expeditionary force in 1801, used European military and economic techniques to make himself omnipotent at home and a threat to his master in Istanbul. He ultimately failed to unseat the sultan, but he won for his descendants the hereditary right to rule Egypt. Sultan Abdülhamit II, the paranoid "Red Sultan" who ruled the Ottoman Empire from 1876 to 1909, pioneered techniques of internal spying and oppression that flourish today in the tyrannies of the Middle East. Relying on these techniques to quell dissent, the nonmonarchical strongmen of today base their unlimited power on elections in which they face no opponents, and aspire to Muhammad Ali's achievement of passing their positions on to their sons. Bashar al-Asad succeeded his father Hafiz in Syria. Saddam Hussein was grooming his sons Uday and Qusay for the succession in Iraq. Husni Mubarak promotes his son Gamal as the leader of the new generation in Egypt. This series of would-be dynasts is matched, of course, by the real dynasts of Morocco, Jordan, Saudi Arabia, and the states of the Persian Gulf. Whether hereditary by right, hereditary by might, or simply a usurpation by military or single-party strongmen, the power of rulers has inexorably strengthened throughout the Middle East over the past two centuries. And the rulers have with few exceptions been fixated upon personal aggrandizement rather than self-sacrificing public service.

So something did go right—again at a personal level. The rulers wanted more personal power, and they got more personal power. The so-called despotisms of the eighteenth-century Islamic world pale in totalitarian control beside the police-state governments of the late twentieth century. And today's media-powered cults of personality, exemplified by omnipresent pictures of the ruler, exceed by far past impositions upon the nation of a ruler's personality. Ottoman coins bore the ornate, and almost unreadable, signature of the sultan; but his facial features were unknown to most of his subjects. No ruler in the modern history of the Middle East remotely resembles the self-abnegating, dutiful, and aloof Meiji emperor, even though worldly aware Turks and Arabs consistently looked upon Japan, from 1905 onward, as a model of successful confrontation with Europe.

## Sharia vs. Sultan

In the case of Meiji, lifelong immersion in Confucianist thought conditioned the emperor to be the servant of his nation—albeit a semi-divine iconic servant—rather than an exploiter of his nation or a power-crazed autocrat. The remainder of this chapter will argue that the worldviews of Arab and Muslim rulers have been as conditioned by Islamic political traditions as Meiji's outlook was by his Confucian upbringing. I do not mean by this that because they were Muslim, they behaved badly in power or fell prey to the evil machinations of Muslim religious figures. My argument, rather, will be that the historic relationship between state and religion that in the Christian wing of Islamo-Christian civilization culminated in an ideology of peaceful (and sometimes not so peaceful) separation, developed in the Muslim wing into a malignant rivalry in which personal tyranny, accompanied by suppression of critical religious voices, developed as a self-fulfilling prophecy.

Traditional Islamic political thought had a horror of *fitna*, a word signifying upheaval and disorder and embracing everything from riot to civil war. Anarchy was intolerable, government a societal necessity. On the other hand, the impulse of rulers to maximize their power to the point of tyranny, *zulm*, appeared as a natural concomitant of government. All that restrained rulers from acting as tyrants was Islamic law, sharia. Since the law was based on divine rather then human principles, no ruler could change it to serve his own interests. Since the interpretation of the law was the prerogative of the ulama, the religious scholars, rulers who were tempted to go beyond the law, and thereby achieve absolute power, had to devise ways of coopting, circumventing, or suppressing the ulama.

This portrayal needs little elaboration in its broad outline. Scholars more or less agree on it. The Turkish historian Halil Inalcik traces it back to a "circle of justice" in pre-Islamic times, citing the words of a sixth-century Persian shah, apocryphally quoted by an early Muslim chronicler: "With justice and moderation the people will produce more, tax revenues will increase, and the state will grow rich and powerful. Justice is the foundation of a powerful state." Then, from one of the earliest Turkish works on statecraft, dating to the eleventh century: "To control the state requires a large army. To support the troops requires great wealth. To obtain this wealth the people must be prosperous. For the people to be prosperous the laws must be just. If any one of these is neglected, the state will collapse."[8]

The Muslim version of the circle of justice sees the sharia as the guarantee of that justice. Even Bernard Lewis, with his generally negative outlook on Islamic traditions, acknowledges the strong association of the sharia with justice and opposition to tyranny. "Westerners have become accustomed to think of good and bad government in terms of tyranny versus liberty. . . . For traditional Muslims, the converse of tyranny was not liberty but justice. Justice in this context meant essentially two things, that the ruler was there by right and not by usurpation, and that he governed according to God's law, or at least according to recognizable moral and legal principles."[9]

The use of freedom as a metaphor has been a staple of European political rhetoric ever since Herodotus celebrated the Greeks' escape from metaphorical "enslavement" by Xerxes' invading Persians. What underlies the metaphor changes over time, however. The Greeks wanted to retain the independence of their city-states. As slave-holders themselves, however, they knew perfectly well that becoming subjects of the Persian emperor would not have been the same as slavery. Two millennia later, "liberty" was still a codeword. Patrick Henry's cry of "Give me liberty, or give me death!" protested the British crown's financial exactions, not indentured servitude. Even more recently, in echoing Moses' "Let my people go," Dr. Martin Luther King, Jr. had in mind an equality of social and economic opportunity that tragically had not accompanied statutory emancipation. And the "Free World" of Cold War rhetoric equated absence of freedom with communist one-party rule, even though many parts of the Free World lived under non-communist one-party rule, dictatorship, or absolute monarchy.

What, then, is the indispensable "justice" of Muslim political theory to be compared with if "liberty" is such a variable metaphor? Some key episodes in the history of democracy's rise in Europe and

North America direct our attention to taxation. "No taxation without representation" was not so resounding a war cry as Patrick Henry's, but it reflected a concrete reality. Britain's American colonies resented being taxed by a parliament that did not represent them. A decade later, it was France's turn. Louis XVI summoned the unruly parliament that touched off the French Revolution because he needed to raise funds.

Tax revolt, of course, can go only so far in explaining rebellions against legitimate authority. Unlike "freedom," however, but like "justice," it is concrete. People experience tyranny in particular forms—financial exactions, injustices—and look for a means of resisting. If the tyranny is starved for money, withholding permission to tax can be effective. If it is starved for soldiers in wartime, as czarist Russia was during World War I, mutiny and desertion can bring it down. When a populace speaks out in opposition to tyranny, regardless of the cultural context, it uses the tools that stand the best chance of achieving a positive result. In the Islamic cultural context, an appeal for justice, and particularly justice rooted in the sharia, is more often than not the tool of choice.

What is supposed to make an appeal to justice work, according to Muslim political theory, is the fact that all Muslim rulers must abide by the same divine ordinances that are incumbent on other believers, and they must uphold those laws in their governance. In addition, as we saw in the preceding chapter, the rulers must recognize that the interpretation of the laws in judicial proceedings is the job of the ulama, a body of religious specialists that originated outside the orbit of government control. The pre-Islamic circle of justice saw justice as depending on the moral character of the monarch, thus raising Juvenal's incisive query: *quis custodiet ipsos custodes?* ("Who watches the watchmen themselves?") In Islamic political theory, the theoretical assumption is that, in fact, there *is* someone other than the rulers themselves monitoring the rulers: the ulama.

Sadly, as every historian of Islam knows, in practice the ulama seldom succeeded in preventing despotism. For the post-1500 period, contemporary chronicles of the Turkish (Ottoman), Iranian (Safavid), Indian (Mughal), and Moroccan (Saadian) monarchies abound in stories of arbitrary killing, licentiousness, internecine outrages, and the like. Leading ulama, as often as not coopted by the ruler's money, seem to have weighed very little as a moral counterweight. On the other hand, examples are hard to find of ulama becoming the prime facilitators of royal domination after the fashion of seventeenth-century European churchmen like Cardinal Richelieu and Cardinal Mazarin, who as chief ministers paid scant attention to religion in governing France for Louis XIII and Louis XIV. On those rare occasions when Muslim monarchs do seem to be subject to religious guidance, as under the first Saudi regime in eighteenth-century Arabia, religious concerns appear to take priority over despotic whim.

A litany of despotic acts in the face of a theoretical, but seemingly impotent, countervailing force in the hands of the ulama tells only part of the story, however. Muslim rulers have unjustly had their sons strangled, their viziers decapitated, and compliant stable-boys raised to the highest posts in government. But tyrannical acts like these are not the concern of the ordinary populace or of the theoretical circle of justice. Just as today in America, for most people, justice means knowing that there is a stable and consistent body of law to which one can turn for protection or redress, and believing that the officials administering that law are fair and impartial. The personal moral behavior of a president may arouse a certain morbid fascination, but justice does not depend on it. By the same token, in traditional Muslim societies, concerns for justice focused not on royal caprice, but on a religious court system staffed by ulama.

The twentieth-century sociologist Max Weber, extrapolating perhaps from received European opinions about oriental despots, coined the term "qadi justice" (referring to the judge presiding over a Muslim court) to describe the utmost in arbitrariness of judicial procedure.[10] However, scholars who have gained access to the judicial court records of the Ottoman Empire, unavailable in

Weber's day, have thoroughly and repeatedly refuted this stereotype. Minutely studying case after case, they have shown that justice was generally meted out impartially, irrespective of religion, official status, gender, or ethnicity. Clear indicators of the perception that the qadi's court was in fact a place where justice could be found are the legal disputes involving two Jews or two Christians. Not being subject to the sharia, Jews and Christians were free to go to their own religious authorities for adjudication of disputes; but in many cases they went instead to the qadi. In these cases the qadi served essentially as the judge of a civil court. In addition, close study of the way in which judges reached their decisions reveals not arbitrariness, but careful and thoughtful study of precedent, consultation of standard legal treatises, and application of a time-honored system of legal logic.

Looking at Islamo-Christian civilization at large, the struggle of monarchs to expand their personal jurisdiction and limit religious jurisdiction is a common feature. In Latin Christendom it gave rise to repeated conflicts between the crown and the church from the Investiture Controversy of the eleventh century to the Peace of Westphalia of 1648 that brought peace between Catholics and Protestants by curtailing the extension of jurisdictional claims beyond national boundaries. In judicial matters, the kings bested the priests.

In the Muslim world, the priests (ulama) were weaker, but they held their own. The century and more of Mongol rule inaugurated by Genghis Khan's invasion in 1218 accustomed the subject populations to accepting a ruler's decrees as law. Each decree was called a *yasa*, leading some Muslim observers to believe that the Mongols had an entire code called the *Yasa* equivalent in scope and character to the sharia. Though the Genghis Khanid dynasty that ruled Iran converted to Islam long before its last sultan died in 1335, the various Mongol and Turkic warlords—Muslims all—who fought over the remnants of his empire continued to revere the family of Genghis Khan as a touchstone of legitimacy and continued to issue legal decrees. The Mongolian word *yasa* became equated with the Arabic word *qanun* (taken ultimately from the Latin word "canon"), and the issuance of qanuns, or edicts, became a sufficiently normal part of post-Mongol imperial rule for the Ottoman sultan known in the west as Suleiman the Magnificent (r. 1520–1566) to be lauded by his subjects as Suleiman Kanuni, Suleiman the Lawgiver.

If any of the caliphs of Baghdad had been vouchsafed a glimpse of a future that included such acknowledgement of sovereign legislation, they would surely have been amazed at the implied erosion of religious jurisdiction. They too had issued edicts, usually, like the Ottoman sultans, with the goal of raising money; but their decrees had always been considered disreputable contraventions of religious law. Newly installed rulers sometimes advertised their cancellation of the illegal laws of their predecessors. Like the European monarchs, then, the shahs and sultans of the post-1500 era strove to increase their legislative authority; but in the absence of a religious cataclysm like the wars of religion between Protestants and Catholics, the Islamic legal system held firm. Lacking legitimate grounds for establishing royal courts that would compete directly with those dominated by the ulama, the rulers settled for cooption. They funded and built elite seminaries (madrasas) and exercised their prerogative of appointing judges (qadis) and legal advisors (muftis). In matters of highest state policy, this produced in most cases a gratifyingly compliant judiciary, but it did not diminish the theoretical or practical dominance of the sharia, particularly in the eyes of the ruler's subjects. Nor did it wean the justice-seeking populace from looking to religious courts, presided over by ulama, for succor. As they had for centuries, the people continued to look for leadership to the ulama, large numbers of whom were trained in seminaries that were not under government control.

How aggravating for a would-be tyrant—or later a would-be modernizer. Though the ruler's hands were normally free, the manacles of the religious law were in plain sight, just waiting for him to go too far. Within the cultural discourse of Islam, there seemed to be no way of eradicating this theoretical opposing force.

## Reform and Resistance

The French Revolution and its Napoleonic epilogue punctured the universe of theoretical Muslim discourse that had for so long postulated a dynamic tension between tyranny and sharia. The French occupation of Egypt after Napoleon's invasion of 1798 was short-lived. The invader's pamphlets proclaiming a French objective of liberating the Egyptians from the tyranny of their rulers were met with ridicule. And the robust international market for Egyptian wheat created by wartime conditions collapsed after Waterloo. But the French emperor's omnipotence and grandeur, along with his establishment of the Code Napoleon as the law of the land, and his reaffirmation of the anticlerical attitude spawned by the French Revolution, provided for Muslim rulers a vision of what a true tyrant might accomplish using modern European methods. For a decade and a half, Napoleon commanded the attention of every political personage on both sides of the Mediterranean. Like Adolf Hitler in the twentieth century, he loomed larger than life, and his deeds could not be ignored, even in Muslim lands.

The history of post-Napoleonic efforts to maximize state power, inaugurated by Muhammad Ali and Sultan Mahmud II and continued by their respective successors, has been retold many times with little recognition of how they parallel what was simultaneously transpiring in Europe. The model for such studies is Bernard Lewis' *The Emergence of Modern Turkey*. While narratives of change in Europe focus on the revolutions of 1830 and 1848, and the royalist efforts to oppose them led by the Austrian Prince Metternich, narratives of change in the Muslim world concentrate more materially on programs to bring armies and navies up to European standards by introducing new armaments and training: factories for uniforms and arms; military schools for instructing officers in gunnery, medicine, and military music; compulsory army service for common citizens; and economic measures, such as state monopolies, to pay the costs.

Such programs required ambition on a Napoleonic scale and a willingness to destroy the old to build the new. Muhammad Ali slaughtered the Mamluk slave-soldiery that had dominated Egypt for centuries, and then sent his own Albanian troops to fight a long and draining war against the Saudi kingdom in Arabia. This effectively cleared the decks for creating a completely new army. Mahmud II slaughtered the soldiery of his own Janissary Corps in 1826 to remove the greatest obstacle to imitating Muhammad Ali. Both men turned to European arms, European military advisers, European instructors for their new military schools, and the dispatch of prospective officers and administrators to Europe for training in modern sciences and instruction in European languages.

In what would be a preview of the American campaign against Saddam Hussein in 1991, in 1840 the European powers pulled Muhammad Ali's teeth after he became too threatening to the Ottoman sultan, a neighbor whom the European powers were unwilling to see fall. They demanded, and after initial resistance accomplished, a substantial disarmament and a dissolution of the economic monopolies—regime change—that had sustained the previous build-up. Seeing the direction the wind was blowing from, Ottoman officials involved in Mahmud's rival military renewal—warmly encouraged by European ambassadors—agreed that "reforms" were needed in nonmaterial areas as well. Over the following decades, through the mechanism of imperial edicts, they introduced law-codes constructed on European models and European-style judiciary practices. High schools with curricula that stressed science and European languages were established to feed into the military officer schools. And in 1876, an Ottoman constitution was promulgated and an elected parliament convened—only to be suspended almost immediately by Sultan Abdülhamit II.

The principle of religious equality between Muslims, Christians, and Jews, pushed particularly strongly by the European ambassadors, made steady headway throughout the period.

The entire movement, termed "renewal" (*tajdid*) in Arabic and "reorganization" (*tanzimat*) in Turkish, is labeled "reform" by some historians, "Europeanization" or "Westernization" by others. But since every aspect of it was paralleled by contemporaneous developments in certain European countries, most notably Russia, there is little reason to separate it from the overall currents of change, and resistance to change, that beset Islamo-Christian civilization as a whole in the aftermath of the Napoleonic upheaval. What separating the Muslim from the Christian political sphere fosters is the retrospective imagining of a historical goal, that goal being Muslim self-improvement aiming at a standard of civilization set by the West.

From the point of view of historians of the modern Middle East, that goal was never reached. "Reform" failed to turn the Ottoman Empire into a part of Europe. Far from gaining the respect of the Europeans, between 1830 when the French occupied Algeria and 1920 when the League of Nations subjected the Arab provinces of the fallen Ottoman Empire to European occupation under the mandate system, every part of the Middle East and North Africa, except Turkey, succumbed to European imperial domination.

However, the master narrative of Europeanizing "reforms" and their failure is not the only way of looking at the long-term results of the post-Napoleonic upheaval in the Middle East. As in Europe itself, new techniques and practices, such as state-controlled telegraphic communication, railroad lines, military conscription, and systematization of bureaucratic practices progressively enhanced authoritarian control. The suspension of parliament by Abdülhamit II (r. 1876–1909) reads as a tragic failure of reform when looked at with the goal in mind of achieving parity with Europe, but the sultan's authoritarianism was right in step with Bismarck, Napoleon III, and Czar Nicholas II, as was that of the dictatorial triumvirate who seized power from the sultan in 1908, ostensibly to restore the Ottoman constitution. Even Mustafa Kemal Pasha (later Atatürk), who saved Turkey from foreign occupation following World War I, and who was undoubtedly sincere in his hope that Turkey would someday become a fully European state, resembled Lenin, Stalin, and Mussolini in his resort to authoritarian practices.

The Muslim road to authoritarianism, however, differs significantly from that in Europe. Prospective European dictators, as well as hereditary absolute monarchs, had to contend with strong public movements for constitutional government and electoral institutions, but the Christian churches supported the rulers' authoritarian tendencies more often than they opposed them. The opposite obtained in Muslim lands. Resistance to government "reforms" centered among the ulama. Historians who interpret the Europeanization movement as the Muslim world's sole, and ultimately forlorn, effort to catch up with the West see this resistance as obscurantist and obstructive. How, after all, could the Muslims enter the modern world with a benighted, backward-looking clergy dragging them down? This viewpoint, which is certainly not without merit in certain cases, considers the steps that would-be dictators took to undermine the foundations of ulama influence fully justifiable, given the need to free the government of their clerical stranglehold. Whether sharing this viewpoint or withholding judgment on the reformers' anticlerical measures, historians all agree that the reforming governments saw organized ulama power as endangering their designs.

The question in terms of interpretation is: 1) whether the ulama opposed reforms because they were against modernity, a view that finds the most supporters today; 2) whether they opposed them because they were part and parcel of a governmental attack on their own well-being and social status; or 3) whether they opposed them because they saw them facilitating the growth of tyranny. The first two alternatives certainly go far toward explaining the motivations of the ulama in many instances. But opposition to tyranny cannot be easily dismissed. It is incontrovertible that ulama and laymen of deep religious conscience played leading roles in some of the best known episodes of opposition to domestic tyranny. The Iranian Tobacco Rebellion of 1891–93 developed when the shah granted a monopoly on the production and sale of tobacco to a British entrepreneur. High-ranking ulama responded to the complaints of Iranian tobacco merchants by pronouncing a ban on smoking. The ban was so effective that the shah was forced to cancel the concession. In another instance, the Arab uprising against the Ottoman Empire during World War I was led by Sharif Husain, the descendant of the Prophet, who was known to pilgrims throughout the Muslim world because of his position as governor of Mecca and Medina. Powerful religious opposition also developed when Atatürk abolished the caliphate in 1924 in favor of his personal dictatorship. Religious figures from many countries came together in several international conferences to call for its restoration.

Religious scholars and Sufis also assumed leadership of numerous movements resisting foreign domination. A charismatic religious figure presenting himself as the Mahdi, or Messiah, led the opposition to Anglo-Egyptian control of the Sudan in the 1880s. Palestine's grand mufti (chief jurisconsult), Hajj Amin al-Husaini, took command of Palestinian resistance to Zionist settlement. And a Sufi of the Naqshibandi brotherhood named Shaykh Shamil fought tenaciously against Soviet expansion in the Caucasus.

Irrespective of the protagonists' attitudes toward modernity and reform, these acts of religiously led resistance testify to the continuing potency of Islam as a bulwark against foreign and domestic authoritarian rule. Muslims in distress accepted the notion that men of religion should lead them. To be sure, resistance to dictatorship by individuals of deep religious conscience is not unknown in Europe. But priests did not lead armies, bishops did not anathematize dictators, and popes did not ban smoking. Europe's Christians had long since shifted from looking to the church for protection against tyranny to looking to political leaders working within, or for the establishment of, constitutional or parliamentary institutions. Such was the long-term consequence of the centuries of conflict between church and monarch that culminated in the devastating wars of religion in the seventeenth century. The Christian clergy were tamed and henceforward served as tribunes of the people only in local matters. By comparison, in Islam, the legal authority of the ulama emerged intact from the sea-change of the middle centuries. Despotic shahs and sultans routinely flouted it in their personal lives, but no one dared deny his theoretical subjection to the sharia. As for the common people, Muslim populations that had long looked to the ulama or to saintly Sufi shaykhs as tribunes of justice continued to do so. This was the natural locus of resistance to tyranny and a long-standing part of the political culture.

## Anticlericalism: Success or Failure?

This is not to say, however, that the efforts of the Westernizing governments to undermine the ulama were ineffective, or even that they were unwarranted in the context of changing social and political values. My intention is not to maintain that the ulama were more enlightened than they were. I am simply observing that when a Muslim community feels threatened, looking to religious leaders for help is an ingrained characteristic of traditional Islamic political culture. This explains why so much state energy came to be expended in pursuit of anticlerical objectives, objectives mislabeled "secular" by most western observers. The reforming rulers and their advisers believed that the goal of achieving parity with Europe could not be reached without first maximizing autocratic power, and that meant eviscerating the oppositional potential represented by the sharia and the ulama. In terms of Islamic political theory, what subsequently happened was what was supposed to happen. *Theory predicted that rulers freed from the bonds of the sharia would seek absolute power, and they regularly lived up to that expectation.* By the 1960s most governments in the Muslim world had become "secular" dictatorships. As for the ulama guardians of the sharia, who were theoretically expected to defend against tyranny, their power to act (though not their inclination) was severely curtailed. This new imbalance in the traditional power equation resulted from rulers following the "Napoleonic method," if that term can be used for authoritarian rule based on new military and communication technologies, anticlerical principles, and appeal to the higher goal of becoming a modern society. Unrelenting state suppression of religion as a political force raised the hope that Europe might someday recognize the "secular" Muslim countries as equals, a hope still vigorously alive in Turkey. But anticlericalism also stripped a political culture based on the circle of justice of the one recognized force that in extreme cases could be summoned to resist a slide into tyranny.

Narratives of "reform" give little space to the dislocation of the sharia and marginalization of its guardians. Being typically western in outlook and convinced that living and thinking like Europeans was an appropriate goal for nineteenth- and early-twentieth-century Muslims, the historians who hatch these narratives tacitly affirm that omelets cannot be made without breaking eggs. The only flaw they see in the Europeanization movement is its ultimate descent into unbridled tyranny. This failure, which ironically only became generally recognized after 9/11 when religious resistance to westernized Muslim dictatorships, and to the western governments that supported them, broke with murderous force upon the world stage, was no accident. It was built into the process of Europeanization from the very start.

Someone writing within the traditional discourse of Islam would craft a very different narrative of the last two centuries. The modernizer sees Muhammad Ali's seizure for state use of the vast revenue-generating properties that generations of pious Egyptians had donated for the upkeep of mosques, seminaries, and local public services as an astute means of gaining the resources needed to finance reform. The traditionalist would lament the loss of religious and public services, and the loss of control and jobs by the ulama. The modernizer sees the Ottoman sultans' promulgation of law codes based on European models as progress toward a freer and more equitable civilizational standard. The traditionalist would mourn the abandonment of the sharia and the ulama's loss of control, jobs, and public dignity. The modernizer takes the new state schools emphasizing science and European languages, and the simultaneous closure or shrinkage of seminaries, as evidence of modern thinking on the rise. The traditionalist would see only a decline in religious knowledge, a further shrinkage of ulama opportunity and prestige, and a loss of religiously trained personnel in government service. One can imagine similarly polarized interpretations of the restrictions Europeanizing governments placed on Sufi brotherhoods and Sufi-linked craft guilds, of their redesigns of cities along European lines at the expense of local neighborhood unity, and, in Atatürk's Turkish Republic, of the successful substitution of the Latin alphabet for the Arabic alphabet.

The anticlerical intent of the self-described reformers is clear. But was it successful? Looking at the disappearance and degradation of seminaries and the confining of the sharia to matters of family and personal status in country after country, the answer would have to be yes. But what about the hearts and minds of the Muslim citizenry? Some evidence indeed points to a steady erosion of religion as the touchstone of public life. Other evidence, coming primarily from the second half of the twentieth century, points to the persistence of a political culture based on a tense balance between religion and state and an enduring popular acceptance of religious leaders—albeit leaders of a new type, as will be discussed below—as opponents of tyranny.

The first body of evidence, that indicating an ebbing of religion as a focus of public life, can be seen in a comparison of data from Massachusetts, Turkey, and Iran. Graphs 1–3 show similar declines in parents giving their sons religious first names in all three regions. The first graph, based on the names of Harvard graduates, reflects the naming practices of prosperous families in Massachusetts. The second tallies the names of members of the Turkish parliament and their fathers. The third combines data from provincial cities in Iran.

1 Frequency of names derived from the Old Testament among Harvard Graduates

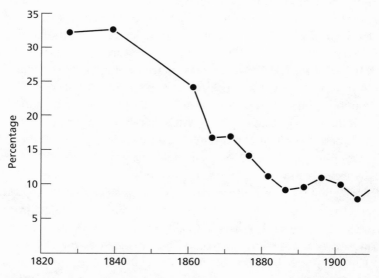

2 Frequency of names Mehmet, Ahmet, and Ali in families of Turkish parliament members.

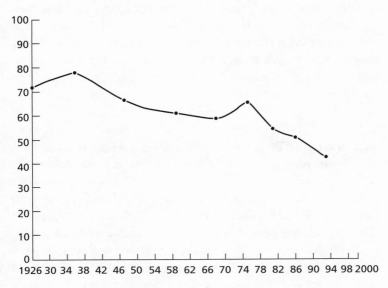

3  Islamic names from Hamadan and Arak (Rajabzadeh)

In each case, the beginning of a steady decline in the popularity of religious names coincides with a strong secular assertion of collective identity: the onset of republican revolutionary ferment in the 1770s in Massachusetts, the beginning of the tanzimat reform movement in 1839 in Turkey (the Ottoman Empire), and Reza Shah Pahlavi's advocacy of Persian nationalism and condemnation of traditional religious practices, such as the complete veiling of women, in Iran in the early 1930s.

Consider the many influences that come into play in naming a child: family custom, remembering a deceased relative, adulation of a public figure, honoring a friend or mentor. Complex and personal factors like these determine many names; but their influence remains more or less constant over time. They cannot explain sweeping changes like those on the graphs. Parental expectations regarding the future are subject to broad change over time, however. Parents who think about helping their sons fit into the kind of society they are likely to grow up in give names that reflect their expectations of the future. In this way they reveal their individual appraisals of the trajectory of change they see around them. Large samples of names, therefore, reflect collective guesses about the future being made by parents. As more and more parents visualize a future in which public life does not revolve around religion, they increasingly opt for nonreligious names.

The three graphs show that the American Revolution, the tanzimat, and the reign of Reza Shah all triggered long-term declines in religious naming. In the Iranian case, the decline temporarily reverses in the pre-revolutionary years of the mid-1970s, when Islam became a rallying point for those opposed to the tyranny of Reza Shah's son, Mohammad Reza Shah. This brief resurgence of "Islamic" naming peaked around 1977. Then the decline resumed despite the creation of the Islamic Republic two years later and the great popularity of Ayatollah Khomeini. If this indicator should prove an accurate harbinger of future developments, the Iranian Revolution will ultimately be seen as the point of transition from tyranny to democracy, rather than from secularism to theocracy. And at what speed? Graph 4, which compares the rate at which religious naming is declining in Iran with the historical rates in Turkey and Massachusetts, suggests that Iranian parents are betting on a more secular future at roughly the same rate as their American counterparts did in eighteenth-century Massachusetts. For a fuller exposition of this technique of measuring attitudinal change, see the Appendix on Quantitative Onomastics.

## Print Culture and New Authorities

Against these indicators of religion receding from societal and parental consciousness in response to government attacks on the sharia and on the traditional religious establishment, one must weigh the evidence for the persistence of a political culture in which the association of religion with justice empowers movements that seek to curb tyranny and oppose foreign penetration.

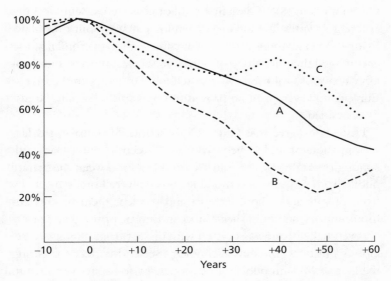

4 Comparison of decline in religious naming in: **A** Massachusetts, **B** Turkey, **C** Iran

(These movements may also seek tyrannical ends of their own design, but they do not advertise such unworthy goals.) Some historians trace the ideological roots of Islamism, to use one of the labels coined for such movements, to the formation of the Muslim Brotherhood in Egypt in 1929; others take their search back to eighteenth-century Arabia, West Africa, India, and Iran. For present purposes, however, the content and genealogy of the various Islamist ideologies are less important than are some new means of communicating them.

Among the many Europeanizing measures aimed at putting the government forever ahead of the ulama, one innovation, the printing press, had the unintended consequence of setting the religious culture of the Muslim world on a new path.[11] Muhammad Ali introduced the first Egyptian newspaper in 1824. Sultan Mahmud II imitated his action in 1831, and the Shah of Iran brought Iran into the print era in 1837. These first publications were essentially government gazettes intended to disseminate news about official activities. Beyond these official newspapers, the governments also encouraged the publishing of books on secular subjects, most notably textbooks for the new state schools. As had been the case in Europe, however, printing proved too powerful a force to be easily contained.

Historians agree that Gutenberg's brainchild transformed European thought and society from the fifteenth century onward. Among other things, the printed word began to wean the literate public from sermons and moral lessons delivered orally by clergy from pulpits and school lecterns and reorient them toward authors, editors, and publishers. Since in Europe printing and printers eventually became associated with dissent from established religious practices, the new technology seemed perfect for curing the literate Muslim public of its propensity to listen overmuch to the ulama. In practice, however, roughly a generation after governmental and secular publications made their first appearance, certain Muslims who were concerned with what was happening to their societies, including a few ulama, began to grasp the potential of the new technology. The result was the slow emergence of a new class of religious authorities who experimented with using the printing press as a pulpit.

Lines of religious authority had for centuries depended on personal classroom linkages between teachers and disciples. Any literate person might read religious texts, but men who did not have a known mentor or a seminary degree commanded little attention in religious circles. Women were totally excluded. With the advent of printing, this changed. Writers, editors, and publishers did not need the credentials provided by a seminary education or the endorsement of an important member of the ulama in order to command an audience. Just as in Europe centuries before, the intellectual monopoly exercised by learned men holding forth in religiously oriented schools and assemblies collapsed in the face of the widespread dissemination of printed materials.

In principle, this is what the Europeanizing innovators desired. It fit well with their other efforts to diminish the influence of the ulama. What they did not foresee was the flood of novel *religious* ideas that began to appear in newspapers, magazines, books, and pamphlets. Just as Protestant authors in sixteenth-century Europe used the newly invented printing press to publish works that contradicted established opinions, so did an increasing number of Muslim religious thinkers. And as in Europe, some of the new authors lacked the traditional seminary education that was the hallmark of the ulama. As the twentieth century progressed, more and more of them came from secular educational backgrounds, being trained as lawyers, doctors, engineers, economists, journalists, and the like. Without the print media, these neophyte religious authorities—the new authorities, as I will call them—would have found no audience. But the transition from a classroom and pulpit culture to a printing press culture made their lack of traditional credentials unimportant. The new technology enabled *authors* to become *authorities* simply by offering the reader persuasive prose and challenging ideas. A Muslim in Egypt could become a devoted follower of a writer in Pakistan without ever meeting him, or meeting anyone who personally knew him, or knowing whether or how he was qualified to write about the faith.

Why did printing cause this transformation? After all, Muslim scholars had produced hundreds of thousands of religious manuscripts over the centuries, and many of them were readily available in mosque libraries or private collections. Yet knowledge acquired from manuscripts lacked the cachet of knowledge acquired in the religious classroom or at the foot of a preacher in the mosque. So how did reading a religious text in print acquire greater import than reading the same text in manuscript? Part of the answer lies in the production of hundreds and thousands of identical copies. One person reading a manuscript and relating its contents to friends and families is a droplet; thousands of people reading and talking about exactly the same text builds toward an ocean. Another part is widespread distribution of these multiple copies.

Whereas lectures and sermons by ulama differ from city to city and country to country, with printed texts, Muslims in South Africa know that they are reading exactly what Muslims in Morocco and Indonesia and Bosnia are reading. In this way the local intellectual communities of ulama trained in seminaries gave way to an international intellectual community of readers of significant books and magazines. We take this for granted as an aspect of Euro-American culture, but we had a four-century head start. In the Muslim religious world it only developed in the late nineteenth century.

Even then the idea that authorship in and of itself might take the place of traditional religious credentials was not immediately apparent. The Arabic religious newspaper *Al-Urwat al-Wuthqa* ("The Firmest Bond," *i.e.*, between man and God [Quran 2:256; 31:22]), published in Paris for 18 issues in 1884, ushered in the new era with its call for an activist reinterpretation of Islamic principles and strong opposition to British imperialism. But its two authors were both trained as ulama: Muhammad Abduh, an Egyptian, and Jamal al-Din al-Afghani, an Iranian who posed as an Afghan to disguise his Shi'ite background. The issues were distributed free throughout the Muslim world until the British banned their import into Egypt (since 1881 under British occupation) and India. Picking up the briefly quenched torch, Abduh's Syrian disciple Muhammad Rashid Rida edited the Arabic-language magazine *Al-Manar* ("The Minaret") in Cairo between 1898 and 1935. Rida had studied in both an Ottoman state school with a "modern" curriculum and an Islamic school, but he wielded his influence as a writer and editor. Thousands of Muslims around the world first encountered the modernist ideas of Muhammad Abduh in the pages of *Al-Manar*. After Abduh's death in 1905, and the subsequent defeat of the Ottoman Empire in World War I, they followed in its columns Rida's own flirtation with nationalism, advocacy of a revived Islamic caliphate, and eventual support for Saudi Arabia as the guardian of Muslim independence in an imperialist world.

*Al-Urwat al-Wuthqa* and *Al-Manar* were both set in type, but Muslim religious writers drew particular benefit from another print technology introduced from Europe. Between 1793 and 1796, a Bavarian playwright named Alois Senefelder, looking for a cheap way of printing his plays, developed a new process he called lithography. When he wetted a flat piece of limestone and inked it, the ink stuck to whatever marks he had made with a greasy crayon, but not to the wet area. Every line, whether alphabetic or pictorial, printed exactly as it had been drawn, and an unlimited number of prints could be pulled from the stone without reducing the quality.

European and American artists hailed this new and flexible way of reproducing drawings, but the innovation of printing books and newspapers by lithography took place outside of Europe and America and became particularly widespread in the Muslim world. Lithographed texts appeared everywhere and became much more popular than typeset texts in Iran, India, and North Africa. The British East India Company brought lithography to India in the early 1820s, and lithographed books soon appeared in Istanbul (1831), Iran (1843), Tunisia (1857), and Morocco (1865). (By comparison, the first lithographic press in the United States started turning out pictures, but not books, in 1825.) Besides allowing elegant Arabic handwriting to be reproduced as written, lithography depended on scribes rather than typesetters. How this affected the control of the publisher, as opposed to the scribe, over the intellectual content of the books he issued has not yet been studied; but it certainly made the technology congenial to the ulama, who were all well trained for scribal activities and who enjoyed reading books that looked like traditional manuscripts.

Authors with western-style educational backgrounds, and little or no traditional religious training, gained increasing prominence after World War II, by which time the most popular, innovative, and inspiring thinkers in the Islamic world were expounding their ideas in print rather than in the classroom. These new authorities effectively supplanted the old authorities, the traditional ulama, whose power had been based on seminary education, judicial office, and income from pious endowments. Sharia judgeships persisted in a few countries, and such seminaries as remained continued to train and employ ulama; but the Muslim public at large, both male and female, increasingly learned about their religion from a torrent of books, magazines, newspapers, and pamphlets, written in large part by people who lacked the credentials to be classified as ulama.

The Iranian revolution revealed the importance of the new, print-based authorities. European imperialist domination in Iran was indirect and late in developing, being formalized only in 1907 through an agreement between Britain and Russia to divide the country into spheres of influence. Thus the strong pressure to impose anticlerical measures and enforce religious equality that the lands to its west had felt from European ambassadors, and later under European colonial administrators, came late to the land of the shahs. This is borne out by the very high rate of religious personal naming that lasted through the 1920s. Delayed exposure to Europeanization also explains why, despite the vigorous anticlerical efforts of the Pahlavi shahs beginning in the late 1920s, Iran lagged far behind Turkey and the Arab lands in marginalizing the ulama. Reza Shah Pahlavi banned the wearing of turbans in parliament and, in 1936, outlawed the figure-shrouding chador. He ordered his police to forcibly tear the garment from women on the streets. Nevertheless, seminaries and shrines remained active and survived various measures designed to undermine their financial independence. At the time of the revolution in 1979, most of the population still looked to the traditional ulama, the old authorities, for guidance. Further buttressing ulama authority was the doctrine in Iranian Shi'ism that every believer should personally follow a leading cleric, called an ayatollah, in matters of faith and behavior.

The Iranian revolution drew much of its force from the popular expectation that the ulama could be turned to for defense against tyranny, an expectation that had previously manifested itself in the Tobacco Rebellion of 1891 and a Constitutional Revolution in

1906. The latter achieved only limited success in curbing the power of the shah, but the constitution it forced into being did contain the seed of ulama veto power over legislative activities. That seed quickly withered only to flower later—whether as a rose or a nettle is a matter of opinion—in the constitution of the Islamic Republic of Iran. Traditional ulama like Ayatollah Khomeini exploited this expectation through the use of new media— books, audiotapes, and television news. They also used traditional means, sending their seminary students to spread their ideas. Non-ulama intellectuals contributed ideologically to the revolution, but lacked the human network of the ulama. Ali Shariati, who was educated in France, galvanized university students with his pamphlets, spellbinding oratory, and novel ideas about Islamic history. The French-educated economist Abolhasan Bani Sadr received Khomeini's blessing as the first elected president of the new Islamic Republic in 1981. He succeeded the provisional government leader Mehdi Bazargan, an engineer also educated in France. All three of these figures gained wide audiences for their writings.

Throughout the Muslim world, displays of Khomeini's portrait signaled, for a few years, sympathy with Islamic revolution. But outside of Iran, and of likeminded circles of Shi'ite ulama in Iraq and Lebanon, very few ulama stepped forward to lead the new current of religious politics. Instead, the new authorities in Turkey and the Arab world included writer-journalists like Egypt's Sayyid Qutb; European-trained lawyers like Mahmoud Muhammad Taha and Hasan Turabi, both of whom founded political movements in the Sudan; engineers like Necmeddin Erbakan, who founded the first significant religious party in Turkey; students of European pedagogy like Abbasi al-Madani, the founder of Algeria's Islamic Salvation Front (FIS), and Rachid Ghannouchi, the founder of Tunisia's Islamic Tendency Movement; and university philosophy professors like Egypt's Hasan Hanafi and Algeria's Muhammad Arkoun, who used western scholarly approaches in developing new thoughts about Islam. The same phenomenon manifested itself in south and southeast Asia.

By the end of the twentieth century, men of deep religious conscience—and for the first time women—had inundated bookstores, newsstands, and sidewalk kiosks with a flood of magazines, newspapers, pamphlets, and books expressing their personal views of Islam. Many publications published *fatwas*, or religious opinions on matters of law and religious practice. Traditionally, such nonbinding opinions came from the pens of high-level ulama. Now they represented the views of the magazine's or newspaper's editors. Some authors called for a return to life as they imagined it had been lived in Muhammad's own time—a matter they did not always agree on—and disparaged the teachings of scholars from later centuries. Others expressed opinions of great novelty, many of them calling for greater personal liberties and the creation of Islamic republics, or at least the participation of Islamic parties in free elections. Still others, most notoriously Osama bin Laden, an engineer, and his associate Ayman al-Zawahiri, a surgeon, preached terrorist violence as the solution to Islam's problems.

## A Message Finds an Audience

In recent decades, the electronic revolution has reinforced the print revolution. Radio and television, being under government control in most Muslim countries, did not initially affect religious authority. But audiocassettes and videocassettes, followed by the Internet, have become effective media for transmitting personal interpretations of Islam. These later technologies do not diminish the historical importance of print because the audiences they found had first been created by the printing press. Yet the use of the new media by the new authorities does serve to underscore another way in which anticlerical measures backfired on the governments that put them in place.

Today's Islamic political revival draws its mobilizing force from three attempts at reducing the power of the ulama that ended up producing unintended consequences. Two have been discussed. First, the marginalization of the ulama, the old authorities, succeeded to a large extent in freeing aspiring authoritarian governments from political threats from their long-term rivals. Today's ulama, at least in many countries, more often than not depend on government salaries and government institutional support, and accordingly defer to the government, or are seen by the general population as deferring to the government, on controversial political issues. However, the unintended consequence of this anticlerical success was to make room for new authorities with different, and less conservative, educational and intellectual backgrounds. Secondly, the print revolution was intended as a vehicle for disseminating governmental views and modern secular and scientific knowledge. It succeeded on both counts. But it had the unintended consequence of handing the rising new authorities a tool for reaching a vast international readership and luring readers away from the declining old authorities.

The third reforming backfire was made by the nationalist governments that emerged after World War II (as well as nationalist Turkey after World War I) when they adopted mass education as a means of training young people for public service and indoctrinating them with secular nationalist principles. They successfully brought about mass youth literacy and political awareness, but with the unintended consequence of creating an enormous audience for the writings of the new religious authorities. Specific conditions in particular countries contributed to a varying time lag between the initial publication of modernist Islamic ideas in the late nineteenth century and the surfacing of Islamist movements as mass political phenomena. The Muslim Brotherhood became a force in Egypt in the 1930s; parallel movements did not appear in Iran until the 1960s. But wherever such movements gained headway, their success depended in large part on youth literacy and a politically aware public.

Political analysts in the early 1980s, belatedly forced by the Iranian Revolution to focus on anti-regime religious movements, often expressed puzzlement at the strength of these movements on university campuses and their special appeal to students in the most competitive and technical programs. Some dismissed the student activists as rebellious teens who would become like their fathers once they matured. Certain others sought more pragmatic explanations: effectiveness of religious movements in arranging study groups for poor students who could not afford to buy copies of the professors' lectures, the security of person afforded to female students who wore Islamic dress, and so forth. Underlying these rationalizations was an unspoken sense that rather than encouraging religious ideas, modern education should have inoculated students against such things. Secularization of society in the West, after all, was historically associated with the role of secular education in refuting hoary religious dicta, from the victory of Copernican astronomy over church-supported Ptolemaic cosmology to the triumph of Darwinism over creationism.

The mass educational systems in the Muslim world also succeeded in transmitting modern scientific views, but they met only limited success in inculcating anticlerical political views. Two characteristic differences between western education and modern education in the Muslim world shed light on this contrast: The latter has always lacked a philosophy of liberal education, and the challenge of teaching about Islam without empowering Islamic scholars has never been resolved.

The educational philosophy of modern education in the Muslim world has various roots. In countries like India, Algeria, and Indonesia, which were subject to colonial rule, modern secular education, more often than not modeled on the system of the imperialist homeland, was usually reserved for a very small number of students from elite families. With high career expectations and a substantial stake in the existing power structure, most of these students were intellectually and politically docile.

In countries like Egypt, the Ottoman Empire, and Iran, which retained their independence long enough to institute their own educational programs, the purpose of modern schools was education for state service, first to train military officers and later to train government officials as well. Though their curricula were European, these institutions were not without indigenous models. The Palace School established in Istanbul by Mehmet the Conqueror in the fifteenth century had trained both officers and administrators, and Egypt had long had training barracks for the Turkish and Circassian slave boys imported for service in mamluk regiments. In both cases, instruction went well beyond military skills. In addition, both in these countries and elsewhere, service in government bureaus relied on apprenticeship training within each bureau. Seminary alumni, who constituted the most numerous group of literate citizens in the nineteenth century, seldom served as military officers or civil administrators. They either became ulama or went into civilian trades.

When modern educators, following the precedents laid down by Muhammad Ali in Egypt and Mahmud II in the Ottoman Empire, took it for granted that government employment was their students' primary objective, they devised curricula for that purpose. They deemed history, philosophy, and literature of little use. Religious instruction they kept at a fairly perfunctory level since they did not want to create a new career track for the ulama. In terms of overall educational philosophy, there was nothing comparable to the notion of liberal arts, or the quest for intellectual broadening for its own sake. Such notions of abstract inquiry as existed were more at home among students training to be ulama, who mostly applied them to religious rather than worldly matters. Exceptions to this pattern were confined almost entirely to foreign religious schools—The American University of Beirut and Istanbul's Robert College founded by American missionaries in the nineteenth century, or the chain of Jewish secondary schools supported from France by the Alliance Israélite Universelle—or western-language preparatory schools like Victoria College in Alexandria and Cairo and The American School in Tehran that received support from western governments. No indigenous private institutions of nonreligious higher education arose to offer alternatives to the secular state schools and the seminaries until the 1980s.

The basic philosophy of education in state schools did not change when independent nationalist governments opted for universal educational in the twentieth century. Students still hoped to work for the government after completing their degree programs, though nationalist fervor and, in some countries, socialist policies made notions of government service less prosaic than those entertained by students in the nineteenth century. Until the 1980s, the Egyptian government would announce each spring how many new graduates it would absorb into its bloated bureaucracy. As the systems grew, instead of small numbers of students from elite families or military castes, thousands of young men and women from humbler social origins packed the lecture halls, and thousands more graduated from high school but failed to gain university admittance.

Educated youth swelled the ranks of the unemployed and under-employed. Their high school or university backgrounds made them more politically aware than the young people in the villages and workshops; their leisure, literacy, and discontent made them avid consumers of religious tracts advocating political activism. In response, apprehensive governments carefully monitored what was being taught in the universities, just as they monitored, or dictated, what was being preached in the mosques. With modern education rooted in traditions of state service, governments had no compunction about interfering in scholarly affairs and limiting freedom of inquiry. Accordingly, the educational systems that had once been the hope of dynamic nationalist regimes began to spiral downward: no classroom freedom, no intellectual innovation, no idealization of the life of the mind, no room in the lecture halls, no jobs for the graduates, and no comparability with parallel institutions in non-Muslim lands. A richer sea for the new religious ideologues to fish in could not be imagined.

## What Went On?

A careful follower of the sinuous course of my argument thus far might now interject that the exception I took to Bernard Lewis' pregnant question "What went wrong?" was quite unfair because

I am adopting the same logic myself. What are unintended consequences, after all, except instances of something going wrong? In
their quest for modernity, equality with the West, and release from
the cold grip of religion, governments diminished the roles and
status of the ulama, introduced printing presses, and established
secular state school systems. They did many other things besides,
but in these three cases the cumulative outcome was to empower
a new and more assertive type of religious authority and create an
audience for it. A classic case of things going wrong: the goals
were clearly visualized, and they just as clearly miscarried.

Yet I would restate my objection to constructing the history of
the last two hundred years in terms of missed goals, because a
sound interpretation of goals and outcomes depends on a much
broader context. To understand why the nineteenth-century architects of change were so single-mindedly anticlerical one must see
their actions in the context of a long-term contest between crown
and mosque over political legitimacy. The ulama were not dis-
credited simply because they were religiously conservative, or the
Sufi shaykhs because they encouraged superstition. Nor would
their hold on the mass of believers have withstood the challenge of
modern ideas if there had been no tradition of mobilizing the
faithful against tyranny and foreign intrusion. In this broader perspective, what went on in the nineteenth century involved not just
the ulama as a reactionary class, but the entire tradition of the
guardians of the sharia as the protectors of justice. One can easily
find different cultural situations—the civil rights movement in the
United States, for example—in which would-be reformers have
looked upon religious leaders as allies rather than enemies.

By the same token, the printing press offered a public platform to
new thinkers of all kinds, and the people I have been calling the new
religious authorities were not the first or the most clamorous in
availing themselves of it. Nationalists, socialists, communists, and
secularists wrote thousands of shelf-feet of books, pamphlets, magazines, and newspapers. They too attracted readers by the eloquence
and logic of their presentations. But the fires lit by these nonreligious ideologies ultimately produced more smoke than heat, and

most of them died out for lack of the crucial combustible represented by people ardently committed to stoking them higher. Print and other new media thus only partly explain the comparative success of the new religious authorities. The more important component of success was their taking the place of the old religious authorities in a political tradition of combatting tyranny with justice. People who followed Hasan al-Banna into the Muslim Brotherhood, or who listened raptly to Ali Shariati denouncing the Iranian monarchy, or who joined Osama bin Laden in al-Qaeda, would have followed a self-proclaimed Mahdi in previous centuries, or a militant Sufi, or a mufti proclaiming his opposition to an act of imperial tyranny. The manifestos of the nonreligious print ideologues ultimately came to naught for lack of roots in an indigenous political culture. The preachings of the religious print ideologues sank deep because the roots were already in place. What went on, then, was not just a media revolution, but a media revolution that favored those who could credibly cite Muhammad as their inspiration over those who took their cues from Voltaire, or Thomas Jefferson, or Karl Marx.

As for mass education, outcomes might have been different if every graduate had found a job in a bustling economy. But perhaps not. Full employment may satisfy material longings, but it does not keep people from chafing under authoritarian rule and suppression of personal freedom, particularly in a world increasingly committed to participatory government. The broader context of what went on was a fulfillment of what Islamic political theory predicted: an increase in authoritarian rule as Islam receded from public life.

In Egypt, Iraq, Tunisia, Algeria, Pakistan, and Indonesia, among other places, the forms and ideals of secular democracy implanted by imperial overlords could not prevent the rise of dictators. Nor in Turkey, the most robust democracy, could the military guardians of Atatürk's secular political vision restrain themselves from repeated coups. In Morocco, Iran, Jordan, and the sheikhdoms of the Persian Gulf, monarchs deployed internal security forces to increase their autocracy, often under the benevolent oversight of western powers that were themselves committed to democratic institutions at home. Even in Saudi Arabia, the bastion of conservative Islam, the power of the royal family, the Al Saud, increased at the expense of the Al Shaikh, the descendants of the kingdom's ideological founder, Muhammad ibn Abd al-Wahhab, and enforcement of religious strictures on public behavior became an instrument of royal social control.

Within the structure of what went on, the rise of Islamic ideologies of resistance should have been predicted. Sharia and tyranny balance each other. As sharia recedes, tyranny increases, until a yearning for a return to a just society—as opposed to a wealthy, powerful, or modern society—causes people to give ear to the guardians of sharia. The idea that this dynamic permanently passed away with the decline of the ulama was wishful thinking based on the historical triumph of crown over clergy in Europe. Islam and Western Christendom are sibling forms of a single civilization, but this does not mean that an evolution of church-state relations that took six centuries to accomplish in Christian Europe could be duplicated in one in the Muslim world.

The lesson of what went on is that Islam cannot be dismissed as a factor in the public and political life of Muslims. To be sure, millions of Muslims live secular lives and deplore religion in politics; but political cultures change only slowly, the wishful thinking of secularists on both sides of the divide between Islam and the West notwithstanding. Railing against Islam as a barrier to democracy and modern progress cannot make it go away so long as tyranny is a fact of life for most Muslims. The ghastliness of international terrorism in the name of Islam, and the bleakness of lives lived under the most oppressive of Muslim behavioral rules, cannot conceal the fact that in rallying Muslims against domestic tyranny and foreign oppression, the new religious authorities, whether peaceful or violent, are acting according to a centuries-old political dynamic designed to protect Muslims from tyranny. Finding ways of wedding this protective role with modern democratic and economic institutions is a challenge that has not yet been met. The path to the future cannot skirt the Islamic past.

*The search for Middle Easterners we could like— because they were like us—put blinders on the Middle East Studies enterprise from the very outset.*

CHAPTER 3

# Looking for Love in All the Wrong Places

IN 1985, CBS television explored turning the novel *Saigon* into a miniseries about American involvement in Vietnam.[1] The British author, Anthony Grey, presented the history of modern Vietnam through the eyes of an American journalist, the scion of a fictitious family intimately involved with Vietnam for over three generations. As the story moved toward the climactic American evacuation of Saigon, the script version highlighted the protagonist's appraisal of the unfolding tragedy: It was *love*, not anticommunism, imperial design, or fear of falling dominos, that had embroiled America in that bloody quagmire. What "love" was supposed to mean was never explained.

It is hard to imagine that an American viewing audience would have fully sympathized with this analysis. (Nor does it surprise that Grey later became a publicist for Claude Rael's theory that life on Earth stems from genetic engineering by space aliens.) Yet Grey's politico-amatory fancy did not entirely lack substance. By comparison with the European imperial powers, America has always seen itself as more altruistic and less greedy, more a provider of help than a grabber of land. Contemporary Americans have come to feel uncomfortable about the brief fever of imperialism that brought Puerto Rico and the Philippines under U.S. control in the Spanish-American War, and they positively recoil at the accusation—on its face, an arguable assertion—of having fresh imperialist designs on parts of the Muslim world. Whatever we have done in remote foreign lands since the end of World War II we attribute either to a quest for security or to basic goodness—Christian altruism repackaged as American idealism.

However, unrequited love appeals only to the most saintly of martyrs. Prior to World War II, American missionaries searched long and hard for Muslims willing to accept the humanitarian American embrace, express thanks for American love and support, and commit themselves to benevolent American ideals and practices. But they encountered frostiness more often than affection once they reached beyond the immediate circle of the sick, the needy, and the ambitious who availed themselves of their medical, charitable, and educational services. After the war, undeterred in their desire to do good, Americans of more secular inclination bent their creative efforts to imagining a deeply appreciative Muslim world, a world capable of requiting American love, and they sought to identify those individuals they were certain were already citizens of such a world. In the process, they blinded themselves to certain realities of Muslim life and thought, and to a growing Muslim suspicion of American benevolence and culture. This chapter will seek to describe postwar thinking about the Middle East and show how the distortions in understanding that it encouraged are still guiding U.S. policy in a post-9/11 world.

## Middle East Studies

*Orientalism*, Edward Said's celebrated critique of western thinking about Islam and the Arab world, focuses on Europeans rather than Americans. It illumines the ways in which travelers, writers, artists, and scholars imagined a lurid Orient of sexual decadence, obscene cruelty, and craven pusillanimity—all, Said argues, with the hidden (or not so hidden) design of justifying imperialism and adding intellectual to colonial subjugation. However, absent American indulgence in establishing colonies, negotiating spheres of influence, and imposing exploitative treaties, the American style of Orientalist imaginings did not particularly suit Said's argument, at least down to the second half of the twentieth century. So the overseas experiences of Washington Irving and Mark Twain in Andalusia and the Holy Land, the pseudo-Muslim exoticism of St. Louis' annual Veiled Prophet pageant, and the lasciviously Oriental hoochy-cooch dance performed by "Little Egypt" at Chicago's Century of Progress exposition, did not command his attention. Nineteenth-century America's fated "other" was the African slave, not the Muslim Arab.

What most Americans knew about Muslims, at least until U.S. soldiers deployed to the far-flung theaters of conflict that made up World War II, came from accounts of the good works of Christian missionaries. Schooling, medical care, relief of misery: such manifestations of Christian love were the American way. Far from supporting imperialism, most Americans who followed the colonial machinations of the British, French, Dutch, and Germans vented feelings of righteous indignation. They shared the European belief in the superiority of Christian civilization, of course; but they did not think that this, in and of itself, justified conquest and colonial subjection.

In the aftermath of World War II, however, a small number of Americans, assisted by a few European scholars, attempted to service new American ambitions to engage with the world by inventing an Orient that was neither Edward Said's sink of slavery, sexuality, and superstition, nor the missionaries' land of unsaved souls. The prominence of Britain's wartime Middle East Supply Centre in Cairo led them to call it the Middle East, a term with an older pedigree but of no previous popularity. The Middle East they imagined centered on a small but mushrooming number of eager, secular Westernizers, men and women who could hardly wait to get on with the business of dragging their benighted brothers and sisters out of their medieval fatalism and obscurantism and into the modern world. Where British travelers had written of noble savages roaming the desert and corrupt effendis lazing about in coffee houses, the new enthusiasts heralded the advent of neophyte democrats, free market entrepreneurs, and secular intellectuals. Where French sybarites had seen sultry demoiselles, postwar American Middle East analysts sketched a near-term future of unveiled women gaining university degrees and important government positions. As with the earlier Orientalist stereotypes, particular individuals who fit these new stereotypes could indeed be found. But the single-minded focus on noble, forward-looking trees obscured, and continues to obscure, any realistic attempt to look at the forest surrounding them.

These imaginings of a new Middle East are the exact opposite of those put forward by the European artists and intellectuals that Edward Said writes about. But lumping them all together as two different faces of Orientalism, while logically plausible, conceals the degree to which American government policies in the Middle East have been driven for half a century by a new vision: Arabs and Muslims that Americans can love and who will love America in return. The postwar American invention of the "modern" Middle Easterner deserves independent consideration because it shaped a distinctly American view of the region, and because it is still a guiding beacon for policymakers.

Bernard Lewis, in the quotation cited in the last chapter, observed that his postwar generation of Americans and Europeans faced the 1950s with minds shaped by the defeat of fascism and the looming Cold War. That same decade saw a select group of American universities establish the first graduate programs in Middle East Studies. The students who populated those first Middle East studies classrooms, myself included, were too young to have experienced the anti-fascist crusade first-hand, but they felt its impact. When we found out how many of our professors had served in the American or British intelligence during the war, we did not question whether wartime experience and postwar anxiety might be shaping the ideas we were being taught more than a dispassionate appraisal of Middle Eastern society, culture, and history.

In the clumsily titled *Ivory Towers on Sand: The Failure of Middle East Studies in America,* a bitter book devoted to disparaging the entire Middle East Studies enterprise, Martin Kramer has argued that the key role in founding this enterprise was played by a cabal of academic entrepreneurs bent on pilfering money from the national treasury, and that government officials assessing America's need for foreign area expertise had nothing to do with it.[2] However, the Middle East was not overlooked in intelligence circles, even if first priority went to the Soviet Union and China, and the moneys provided for the study of the region were not procured on false pretenses.

In 1953, President Eisenhower established the Operations Coordinating Board to succeed President Truman's Psychological Strategy Board. Staffed by representatives of the government's top intelligence, defense, and propaganda agencies, this board sought to understand the aspect of global Cold War competition that would later be described as "winning hearts and minds." In 1957 a working group of the Board issued a classified document entitled *Inventory of U.S. Government and Private Organization Activity Regarding Islamic Organizations as an Aspect of Overseas Operations.* The argument of the report appears in its opening statement on "The Status of Islam Today":

1. **Islam is important to the United States:**

    a. *Because it has compatible values.* The present division of the world into two camps is often represented as being along political lines while the true division is between a society in which the individual is motivated by spiritual and ethical values and one in which he is the tool of a materialistic state. Islam and Christianity have a common spiritual base in the belief that a divine power governs

and directs human life and aspirations while communism is purely atheistic materialism and is hostile to all revealed religion.

b. *The Communists are exploiting Islam.* In spite of basic incompati-
bility, the Soviet and Chinese Communists have far surpassed the
West, including the U.S., in making direct appeals to the Muslims
as Muslims. . . .

c. *It significantly affects the balance of power.* Of the 81 members of the
United Nations, 16 nations have Muslim majorities and there are
32 which have 50,000 or more Muslims . . . [T]he 16 UN members
draw together into a bloc which advances Muslim interests and
may oppose those of the West. But more important is the fact that
Islam is the fastest growing of the world's great religions, due both
to natural increase and missionary activity.

d. *The future direction of Islam is uncertain,* following the negative reaction experienced from the impact of the West and technology on
Muslim countries. Attraction to materialism has undermined
moral and ethical values—leaving many directionless. Intellectuals
in every Muslim land are searching for answers, and unless a reconciliation is achieved between Islamic principles and current social and political trends, the spiritual values of Islam will be lost
and the swing toward materialism will be hastened.

e. *The area covered by Islam is vast.* . . . As a militant missionary faith,
the ultimate aim of Islam is world conversion. . . . In the Middle
East stability ranges from good to poor and where instability pre-
vails, the populace responds most readily to inflammatory appeals.
In Southeast Asia the patterns of modern political and social behavior are in flux but in this region Muslim political parties are
very strong. In blacker Africa Islam is spreading like flame and
large areas may become increasingly receptive to bold anti-foreign
and anti-Western propaganda.[3]

After a few comments on Islamic religious organization, the inventory goes on to identify factors that favor cooperation with the
West—common beliefs, opposition to atheism, natural friendli-
ness toward strangers—and factors that hinder such cooperation,

including Muslim militancy, cultural differences between Muslims and Christians, Muslim resentment of domination by western civilization, Muslim dissatisfaction with democracy, and Muslim feelings of religious superiority.[4] In assessing American capacity to deal with either set of factors, it observes that missionary efforts are of long standing. "The lives of these Christian missionaries created a favorable, admired image of the American in the minds of the Muslims. More recent and extensive contacts have served to bring this image somewhat into question." American businessmen also became engaged in the region, but "tended to carry on business without regard for local religion and culture. . . . There was no effort to relate American business ethics to local ethics and hence to parallel the missionary approach." Such was the state of affairs through the end of World War II.

Until 1946 our legations in the area were staffed by a handful of officers and in several countries we had no diplomatic representative. Since then floods of Americans have gone out as official representatives of this country. *Lacking background they have tended to rely on English-speaking, Western-educated intellectuals and to believe that these locals, and all others, reason and act much as they do.* Few have any idea of the role of Islam in life and society, and they are unaware of the relationship between Islam and the present currents of nationalism and anti-foreignism. Lack of adequate training of American personnel in Muslim beliefs and practices is indicated, for example, by training programs which offer no specific instruction on Islam and by the absence of adequate guidelines to the field which give information on Muslim organizations locally. Leaders of these states do underline the fact that they are devout Muslims and stress that all programs of progress and reform must be in line with the principles of Islam.[5] [emphasis added]

Finally, the inventory makes several recommendations, the most pertinent of which says that "regional studies should be initiated next in the order of Middle East, Africa, and Southeast Asia, or studies on selected countries in these areas."[6] To this end, it lists as resources the fledgling Middle East Studies programs at Harvard, Princeton, the Johns Hopkins University, University of Chicago, University of Pennsylvania, University of Michigan, Columbia University, and UCLA.[7] So Kramer's charge that university programs in Middle East studies came into being solely because a few professors figured out how to winkle money out of the government purse does not stand up to scrutiny.

A look at the substance of the new Middle East Studies programs will cast kinder light on some of Kramer's other contentions, however. The stress on contemporary Islam contained in the Operations Coordinating Board's inventory did not carry over into the universities' Middle East Studies curricula. Also ignored was the warning about "the negative reaction experienced from the impact of the West and technology on Muslim countries" and the caution that without "a reconciliation . . . between Islamic principles and current social and political trends, the spiritual values of Islam will be lost." Instead, as Kramer rightly observes, the Middle East Studies pioneers became committed to theories of "development" and "modernization" that "served as the natural successor of the missionary tradition, and infused Middle Eastern studies [and all other non-Western studies] with an American optimism. . . . So Middle Eastern studies were not only an academic field to be explored; they were also a message to be preached."[8] Where the Operations Coordinating Board was looking for ways to foil the communists, the Middle East Studies professors, like the missionaries before them, were looking for Arabs and Muslims that Americans could love.

## Shaping a Field

Three books written at the close of the 1950s, just as the Board's inventory was being compiled, will illustrate the involvement of Middle East Studies with "development" and "modernization." Not everyone read or assigned these particular works, but everyone knew more or less what they contained, and at least tacitly took their views as gospel.

The first of them instructed students in the irrelevance of Islam. *The Passing of Traditional Society: Modernizing the Middle East,* published in 1958 by MIT professor Daniel Lerner, began with a survey project sponsored by the prestigious Bureau of Applied Social Research of Columbia University in 1950. The survey was administered in Turkey, Lebanon, Jordan, Egypt, Syria and Iran following a trial run in Greece. Three queries preface the 117 numbered questions that make up the survey: Do you ever go to the movies? Do you ever read a newspaper? Do you ever listen to the radio?[9] The remainder of the survey deals almost exclusively with practices and attitudes involved with those media. Exceptionally, question 112 solicits personal data, including religious identity and make of radio. Question 111 asks how often the respondent goes to a place of religious worship and how important religion is in day to day life on a scale ranging from "Very important" to "Not important at all." Religion otherwise goes unmentioned. Five multi-part questions sample specific and comparative attitudes toward the United States, Great Britain, and Russia.

The rationale for the narrow range of questioning, and for what Lerner confesses was a planned overrepresentation of movie-goers, radio listeners, and newspaper readers, rests on an underlying theory that associates exposure to modern media with a transition to modernity.[10] The eminent Harvard sociologist David Riesman observes in his introduction to the book that, "Mr. Lerner's cast of characters puts the Moderns on the one side—they are cosmopolitan, urban, literate, usually well-off, and seldom devout—and the Traditionals on the other side—they are just the opposite. But in between he puts several categories of Transitionals: people who share some of the empathy and psychic mobility of the Moderns while lacking essential components of the Modern style, notably literacy."[11] What exactly "empathy" and "psychic mobility" mean in this context was presumably clear to sociologists of the time.

"The direction of change," Lerner explains, "is the same in all Middle East lands; the secular trend is toward mobility—physical, social and psychic mobility. . . . In every Middle East country the transitional people exhibit more of those characteristics we have already identified with the participant style: urbanism, literacy, media consumption and empathic capacity. . . . The rate of social change everywhere is a function . . . of the number of individuals accruing to the transitional stratum. The more persons who are 'going modern' in any country, the higher is its overall performance on the indices of modernity."[12]

All well and good, except that the outcome of the surveys was cooked in advance. Key indices of modernity were predetermined, with modernity itself being defined according to a specific western model:

Taking the Western model of modernization as a baseline is forced upon us . . . by the tacit assumptions and proclaimed goals which prevail among Middle East spokesmen. That some of these leaders, when convenient for diplomatic maneuvers, denounce the West is politically important and explains why we have chosen to speak of "modernization" rather than "Westernization." Rather more important, Western society still provides the most developed model of societal attributes (power, wealth, skill, rationality) which Middle East spokesmen continue to advocate as their own goal. Their own declared policies and programs set our criteria of modernization. From the West came the stimuli which undermined traditional society in the Middle East; for reconstruction of a modern society that will operate efficiently in the world today, the West is still a useful model. What the West is, in this sense, the Middle East seeks to become.[13]

The theoretical rationale for the book is thus presented as being forced on the author by the declared objectives of the region's "spokesmen" and "leaders." It is reasonable to ask, therefore, who the leaders of that time were.

- Turkey: Following in the footsteps of his mentor, Mustafa Kemal Atatürk, Ismet Inönü served as president of Turkey until political forces led by Celal Bayar and Adnan Menderes, and drawing substantially on religious unhappiness with Atatürk's secularism, defeated his party in an open election in 1950. The Turkish military deposed Bayar and Menderes ten years later and tried and executed the latter.

- Egypt: King Faruq ruled until he was overthrown by a military coup in 1952. Gamal Abdel Nasser quickly emerged as the leader of the coup, and then of the government.

- Iraq, Lebanon, and Jordan: In 1958 a similar military coup overthrew the Iraqi monarchy, headed by the young king Faisal II and his mentor Nuri al-Said. General Abd al-Karim Qasim became Iraq's president. The day after the coup, the president of Lebanon, Camille Chamoun, made an urgent plea to the United States to send troops to protect Lebanon's independence. President Eisenhower complied. Britain and the United States also sent troops to Jordan to protect King Hussein, who had succeeded to the throne after the assassination of his grandfather, King Abdullah, in 1949.

- Syria: Also in 1958, Syria closed out a series of nine presidents and generals that had ruled successively since an initial military coup in 1949 by uniting (until 1961) with Egypt in the United Arab Republic.

- Iran: Mohammed Mossadegh became prime minister in 1951 and gained enormous popular support by nationalizing the Anglo-Iranian Oil Company. Mohammad Reza Shah Pahlavi fled the country in 1953 but soon returned after Mossadegh was overthrown by a coup arranged in part by British and American intelligence services.

The torrid pace of political events during the 1950s makes it evident that the leaders of that era were far more concerned with grabbing or retaining power than with programs to modernize their societies on a western model. Admittedly, however, this may not have been what they said to the American ambassador. Be that as it may, Lerner seems to prefer "spokesmen" to "leaders" in characterizing the people who allegedly set the agenda for how he studied the Middle East. So it may not be fair to speak only of leaders. Besides, although King Faruq clearly did not see eye to eye with Colonel Nasser, nor Inönü with Menderes, nor King Faisal with General Qasim, nor Mossadegh with the Shah, perhaps they did all agree on the criteria for modernization.

Unfortunately, Lerner does not reveal the identities of the "spokesmen" whose views he so deeply respected. It may safely be presumed, however, that they did not include Communist labor leaders, Shi'ite ayatollahs, or the monarchs and shaykhs of the Arabian peninsula. Most likely, the spokesmen consisted of "Moderns," that is, government, business, and educational figures who were committed to closer ties with the West. The Operations Coordinating Board inventory intimates as much when it describes (and deplores) an over-reliance by U.S. diplomats on "English-speaking, Western-educated intellectuals." These individuals affirmed to their American contacts what both parties ardently believed and hoped for, namely, that the Middle East was irrevocably launched on a rapid process of modernization based on the western model. Lerner evidently believed the fantasy that the "Moderns" were about to inherit the earth and designed his study to cloak that fantasy with pseudo-scientific fact.

No one would deny that there were pro-western "Moderns" living in many Middle Eastern countries during the 1950s. Nor can anyone doubt that literacy and media exposure have the effect of changing people's attitudes. What is in question is the trajectory of change. If Lerner had included among his "spokesmen" people like the Egyptian Sayyid Qutb, who became a militant, vocal, and highly literate proponent of revolutionary Islamic activism after a sojourn in the United States in 1948–1950, he would have observed a very different, and deeply anti-western, outlook on modernization. He would have seen the same thing if he had considered the abundant writings of the Pakistani religious activist Abu al-Ala Maududi, which began to circulate in Egypt in 1951. Over the succeeding decades, the views of these and similar Muslim religious activists exerted greater pressure for change than the prognostications of the modernist spokesmen whom Lerner relied on for his study.

This is only one book, of course, but it illustrates three important aspects of Middle East Studies in their formative years: gigantic scale, inattention to Islam, and the assumption that western modernity is the only desirable future.

First, the scale of Lerner's enterprise was immense—six countries speaking three entirely different languages, and the assumption that the entire Middle East was involved in a single historical process. This assumption that modernity is homogeneous contrasted nicely with the similarly popular idea, advanced by the anthropologist Carleton Coon in his widely assigned *Caravan: The Story of the Middle East,* that every traditional Middle Eastern society was a heterogeneous "mosaic" of subnational ethnic, linguistic, and religious groups.[14] As students we learned that tradition was a murky and impenetrable maze, and modernization a straight path to a luminous future.

Secondly, while Islam is ignored empirically in the questionnaire that forms the foundation of the book, Lerner confidently dismisses it as being irrelevant to modernization:

> As the intellectual effort to reformulate Islam in a manner more suitable to modernizing society became inhibited, a psychic gap of serious proportions opened in the Middle East. In some lands, aphasia has gone further than in others. Egypt, to take an extreme case, seems increasingly captive of a false position. Seeking hegemony over the Arab area and primacy among Muslims everywhere, Egypt has sought to erect a unifying symbolism on the majority Arab-Muslim syndrome. But this corresponds poorly to observable reality and provides no guidance to those men-in-motion who most need new words to match their new ways.[15]

Thirdly, western-style modernization is identified without convincing rationale as the conscious goal of Middle Eastern society. No alternative way of engaging the modern world receives serious consideration, nor is any attention paid to the political and cultural critique of the West that grew ever louder from 1950 onward, and was a specific concern of the authors of the Operations Coordinating Board's 1957 inventory.

Yet Lerner does not fit the model of Said's Orientalists. His inventive powers focus on his "men-in-motion," not on romantic tribesmen, steamy harems, or sleazy city Arabs. Lerner devotes most of his attention to describing a type of Middle Easterner that Americans might admire and like. (Anthony Grey would say love.) His Transitionals are modern, western, and on the move. They are so clearly, in Lerner's mind, the people who will shape the future that he scarcely needs mention the exotic Orientals of bygone generations.

From our perspective in the first generation of students engaged in Middle East Studies, the views of Lerner and other members of what we now call "the greatest generation" carried great weight. Ourselves neophytes with little or no prior knowledge of the Middle East, we had no basis on which to criticize what we were taught. Classmates from Middle Eastern countries or from families native to the region were few. On the rare occasions when we did encounter native speakers of Arabic, other than our instructor, the discovery that the classical language learned in class bore scant relation to the everyday spoken language was profoundly dispiriting. Five years of Harvard Arabic and I couldn't express myself in Beirut without causing chuckles!

Yet we were expected to emerge from two years of graduate training with sufficient area expertise to qualify for positions in government or business. The scope of the knowledge deemed pertinent to the field was immense, embracing more than twenty countries, three language areas, and an array of academic disciplines ranging from economics and anthropology to history, political science, and language. What made this impossibly broad curriculum conceivable was the postwar self-confidence of the professors drafted into the task of inventing Middle East Studies, and the all-encompassing utility of theoretical perspectives like

Lerner's. Although Middle East Studies did not enjoy the respect of scholars with deep grounding in the traditional academic disciplines, our esprit de corps was high, as was our trust in the soundness of what we were taught and our unwillingness to find fault with our professors.

A second example of the broad canvas on which the writers of the 1950s sketched their outlines of the Middle East is *The Politics of Social Change in the Middle East and North Africa*, published by Princeton professor Manfred Halpern in 1963. Halpern discusses his methodological approach in a Foreword:

> This study rarely pauses to make explicit the methodological framework of its analysis, or the concepts and hypotheses that underlie its conclusion. . . . It is not based merely on existing facts. It does not say simply, for example, that the Middle East has few political parties, that there is some talk, though less effort, to form a few more, and that it would therefore be premature to estimate just what political parties might be able to accomplish. The book goes further and asks what role parties must play if they are to be effective in creating a new political culture in the midst of rapid social transformation. . . .
>
> We are here exploring some sixteen countries that have experienced similar problems in passing from an Islamic past into the modern age. . . .
>
> The two methods of analysis on which this book chiefly relies can help us to enhance the range, accuracy, and relevancy of interpretation. They cannot compensate for our ignorance of facts, and much of what is said here still rests on selected examples rather than full and complete evidence. Such examples, nonetheless, are intended in every case to be a convincing illustration that data in support of a particular hypothesis do exist. They are offered on the assumption that further research would reveal corroborative evidence in other parts of the region.[16]

Halpern's confession that he takes for granted that the region is in the process of "passing from an Islamic past into the modern age" does not lessen the degree to which he is prepared to manipulate data in envisaging a Middle East that fits his vision of the future. Here is how he addresses the consensus among observers that the region lacks a middle class suitable for leading the way into the modern age, a problem that Lerner solved by discovering, through his survey, various tiers of "Transitionals":

> In our unproductive search for middle classes in underdeveloped areas, the fault has been in our expectations. We have taken too parochial a view of the structure of the middle class. . . . Leadership in all areas of Middle Eastern life is increasingly being seized by a class of men inspired by non-traditional knowledge, and it is being clustered around a core of salaried civilian and military politicians, organizers, administrators, and experts.[17]

Halpern, the social science theorist, joins Lerner, the social science empiricist, in assuming that a process of modernization is underway, and in seeking to identify its leadership elements. Both perspectives looked with guarded optimism on the military coups that rocked the region in the 1950s because they confidently counted on the officer corps—"men on the move" for Lerner or the "salaried new middle class" for Halpern—to blaze a trail of modernization. That the trail would actually lead to police state oppression came as a sad surprise.

Halpern also joins Lerner in affirming the haplessness of Islam:

> As long as the Moslem holds that the comprehensive order revealed by God in the seventh century and subsequently hallowed by tradition is final and cannot be amended, he will be unable to study the world independently and scientifically in order to fashion his own world himself. . . . The Moslem [unlike the Christian] emerges from an age in which tyranny, anarchy, hunger, and death seemed often beyond remedy, an environment helping to reinforce his religious dogma that God was all-powerful, and that the moments of life were not a succession of cause and effect but separate God-created miracles.[18]

While Halpern hints that "a reformation and renaissance are well under way in the Middle East,"[19] he doesn't say what it consists of. Instead, his chapter on contemporary Islam concentrates on the failures of reformist Islam, the triumph of secular leadership, and the threat of neo-Islamic totalitarianism.[20]

The Middle East Studies lecturers of the 1960s, following Lerner, Halpern, and others, taught that Westernization was inevitable. Consequently, it was our duty as students—actually, as a medievalist, I was exempted from this part of the curriculum—to discover ways of studying this miraculous transformation and to identify and help the types of people who were making it happen. That same duty is being preached to fledgling colonial administrators in Iraq today.

Islam, as understood by virtually everybody, appeared at best a historical relic destined to pass away as a component of "tradition." At worst it had a threatening potential for totalitarianism. In either case, Islam was not an approved topic of study, except for medievalists. This theory-based dismissal of any positive view of contemporary Islam contributed substantially to the fact that between the end of World War II and the Iranian Revolution of 1979, scarcely a handful of books on contemporary Islam were written by American-trained scholars. Of those that were written, two dealt with Egypt's Muslim Brotherhood, the foremost example of Islam as threat.

*The search for Middle Easterners we could like—because they were like us—put blinders on the Middle East Studies enterprise from the very outset.* The ideological lenses through which Said's Orientalists once gazed upon a land of exoticism were reground in postwar America to produce a differently distorted vision of men-on-the-move. Invisible between the two imaginative constructions lay other alternatives that proved in time to be more important. The middle ground of people deeply wedded to their religious traditions, but eager to share in at least some of the benefits of the modern world, gave birth to the Iranian Revolution, a multitude of Islamic movements and political parties, and, sadly, the jihadist plots of Osama bin Laden. But with rare exception, Islamic activism went unobserved and unanalyzed in the early days of Middle East Studies, and remains disturbingly puzzling to the present day.

The exaggerated role that modernization played in postwar thinking stemmed from the idea that capitalism, calling itself "the free world," was destined to compete worldwide with communism in offering ways of becoming modern. In the Middle East case, the inventory by the Operations Coordinating Board portrayed the world of Islam as both a spiritual and material battlefield in the Cold War. John C. Campbell's *Defense of the Middle East: Problems of American Policy*, published in 1958, drove this lesson home for students of Middle East studies.[21] Campbell was the Director of Political Studies of the Council on Foreign Relations, a venerable New York institution long associated with sober and liberal assessments of world problems. His book reflects the deliberations of a Council study group that included virtually all of America's Middle East political scientists of the pioneer generation.

Like Lerner and Halpern, Campbell's field of view encompasses the entire Middle East, but his focus is on countering Soviet imperialism. Modernization is assumed, but not emphasized: "Still, the stirrings of every one of the Middle East nations reflect an urge that goads them all: the urge to build a new society, to take their place in the modern world, without becoming the instruments of others or losing their national and cultural identity in the process."[22] Campbell's view of Islam similarly subordinates it to his main theme:

> Certainly Islam cannot be counted upon to serve as such a barrier [to Soviet expansion]. The theory that communism and Soviet influence could never make inroads in the Moslem world because they are materialistic and atheistic has not been borne out. Religion does have a significant place in Middle Eastern society. It colors both popular and official attitudes. But it does not establish an absolute immunity to a political virus such as fascism or communism. Communist theo-

ry does have certain superficial parallels with Islamic dogma, and the promise of a better material life is not inconsistent with it. Above all, the impact of the modern world on Islam has produced two major trends which tend to open the door to Communist influence: first, the inability of traditional doctrines and institutions to hold the loyalty of the intellectual leaders and the new generation bent on finding a way out of material backwardness; and second, the revulsion against the West which, while often reinforcing the sense of dedication to Islam, has often created also a sense of identification with whatever theories and political forces were hostile to the West.[23]

Despite their tunnel vision, the three works described above, along with a handful of others, including Bernard Lewis' *The Emergence of Modern Turkey* and Carleton Coon's *Caravan*, add up to a major intellectual accomplishment. Their grand and tendentious theories and generalizations laid the foundation for a Middle East Studies enterprise that otherwise would have floundered. Applauding the founders of the field for their enterprise and audacity, however, cannot conceal the fact that the limitations and unreality of some of their ideas continue to distort American understanding of the Muslim world down to the present day.

## On to Baghdad

Some four decades have elapsed since the publication of these theoretical visions. Wars and revolutions, oil shocks and peace processes, terrorist bombings and *intifadas,* have come and gone, each dramatic event buffeting the community of Middle East specialists in academia and government, and more often than not falsifying the predictions they had put forward in the aftermath of the previous crisis. No one would argue that they got things right more often than they got things wrong. Some of Martin Kramer's fulminations in *Ivory Towers on Sand* hit the mark. Those scholars in the 1980s who (correctly) saw in political Islam a promising route to a democratic future *did* fail to predict the potency of religious terrorism. And those who (again correctly) looked for the emergence of "civil society" as a harbinger of liberal evolution *did* underestimate the tenacity of police-state oppression. What Kramer uncharitably leaves out is the failure of almost all predictions about the Middle East during the second half of the twentieth century, including those visualizing peace and region-wide prosperity arising from Israeli-Palestinian negotiations, those trumpeting the withdrawal of religion from the sphere of public affairs, and those predicting an enthusiastic welcome for American soldiers in Iraq.

Failures in prediction, in Kramer's view, can best be dealt with by terminating government funding for Middle East Studies, and paying greater attention—if that is possible—to the predictions of the think-tank that published his book, the Washington Institute for Near East Policy (WINEP). What might this lead to with regard to Islam? A WINEP "Special Policy Forum Report" dated April 10, 2003 quoted Daniel Pipes, Kramer's colleague and mentor, as saying, "If militant Islam is the problem; moderate Islam is the solution. The world is facing not a clash of civilizations, but rather a struggle between Muslim moderates and militants. . . . The time has come for Washington to encourage democratic development, but in small, gradual steps. This means building civil societies in which the rule of law operates, freedom of speech and assembly develop, local elections take place, and so forth."[24] These recommendations sound suspiciously like the optimistic 1980s attitudes toward moderate Islam and civil society that Kramer attacked in his book as naïve and apologetic.

The failure of hard-won expertise, whether deployed by Middle East Studies professors or by Martin Kramer and Daniel Pipes, to produce more credible and consistent predictions points to fundamental misunderstandings at the very core of the enterprise. To be sure, other explanations for failed forecasts have their appeal. Some maintain that hopeful prospects have repeatedly been derailed by the failure of successive American administrations to give full support to Palestinian aspirations, and to force liberalization on heavy-handed dictators and monarchs. These paths not taken—

in practical terms, perhaps, never more than dreams—may well have made Middle Eastern politics more predictable. A socialization of oil wealth across all the nations of the Muslim world, and a preference for spending it on improving life in petroleum-poor as well as petroleum-rich states, as opposed to squandering untold billions on armaments, might have helped as well. But lamenting lost opportunities contributes little to the ongoing problem of trying to understand the world we face today.

The question is whether we are willing to jettison the assumptions of the 1950s, or whether we will forever be on the lookout for men-on-the-move who can remake the Muslim world in our image. A look at what has been written since September 11, 2001 is not encouraging. It is as difficult today as it was in 1960 to find a point of intersection between American policy and the world-view of tens, if not hundreds, of millions of Muslims who want their governments and the basic institutions of their societies to reflect a Muslim moral and political order. This lacuna does not stem from a paucity of works by Muslims describing and advocating one or another version of such an order. They are legion. Nor are non-Muslim scholars inattentive to Islamic matters in the way they were before the Iranian Revolution. Books offering new looks at Islam—this one included—appear every month. The problem is integrating this mass of information about Islam with the perspectives of those charged with determining government policies. The policy community, and the scholars on its fringes, continue to shun alternative visions of modernity that might embody a Muslim rather than a western perspective. At worst, they posit Islamic politics as a malignant and inveterate foe, debating the best strategies for holding the Muslims at bay while simultaneously whining, "Why do they hate us?" At best, they acknowledge a need to be sensitive to local cultural norms, and even to moderate Islam, without figuring out how such sensitivity can be manifested in practice.

Middle East Studies began, as we have seen, in the shadow of the Cold War. Its birthright included a mandate to search for ways to persuade Muslims to follow the free world route to modernity rather than the garden path to dictatorship proffered by the communists. The fact that the free world path led to dictatorships as bad as any produced by communism—in my view, as expressed in the preceding chapters, a result of the long-term workings of a distinctively Muslim political system—did not invalidate the mandate, because the ultimate goal was the defeat of communism, not the salvation of the Muslim world.

Despite the upheavals that have rocked the region since 1979, the mandate of 1957 has not changed much. The communists are gone, but we are still asking how we can persuade Muslims to follow a western model of modernity. With the disappearance of the competing socialist model of modernization, which was just as western in its roots as the free world model, the alternative today is not "going communist," but becoming a "failed state," or even a "rogue state." Where Cold War thinking embodied a choice of modernization models, post–Cold War modernization offers poverty, chaos, and computer illiteracy as the only alternative. Policy circles seem incapable of imagining a Muslim model of modernity. Ironically, the modernity that emerged in Japan after five years of American occupation was distinctly Japanese. For a brief moment, at the height of Japan's economic boom, some Americans even speculated that it might be a superior modernity. Those who advanced the Japanese occupation as a model for postwar Iraq, however, seem to have baseball, Hello Kitty, and Elvis impersonators in the back of their minds rather than women in headscarves and turbaned mullahs. Western triumphalism clouded our understanding of Japan then just as it clouds our understanding of Islam now. Moreover, our inability to imagine alternative positive futures for a region whose future is increasingly in American hands inevitably vitalizes Muslim charges of imperialism. Like latter day missionaries, we want the Muslims to love us, not just for what we can offer in the way of a technological society, but for who we are—for our values. But we refuse to countenance the thought of loving them for their values.

An observation penned by John C. Campbell in 1958 retains its salience some four decades later:

> We shall have to put much seemingly unnecessary effort into convincing people, who should know as much from what they can see, that Western imperialism is a spent and dying force. We shall have to proclaim, more times than seems sane, our adherence to the principles of national sovereignty and noninterference in the internal affairs of others, and to flatter those who regard these principles as the answer to the world's problems.[25]

A contemporary version of the same sentiment appeared in a 2002 exhortation by John Brown, a veteran U.S. diplomat whose views are shared by other senior diplomats and communications professionals, urging more government investment in public diplomacy:

> In the war on terrorism, for example, public diplomacy's diverse tools can have an enormous impact in the Muslim world. First, a truthful and accurate information campaign, if both persuasive and credible, can set the record straight about U.S. policy and intentions. . . .
>
> Finally, given the lack of knowledge about U.S. culture and the tendency to equate it with violence and pornography, there is a special role for serious, but not solemn, cultural activities pertaining to the United States that would appeal to Muslim audiences, especially the young.[26]

The warning about "the negative reaction experienced from the impact of the West and technology on Muslim countries" contained in the Operations Coordinating Board's 1957 inventory retains its salience as well. The problem is not the technology. No group is more assiduous than Osama bin Laden's jihadists in exploiting the possibilities opened up by modern media. The problem is the proposition that technology and western social and governmental practices are an indivisible package. On this score, decades of frustration in selling America to the Muslim world have produced a somewhat deeper awareness of Muslim sales resistance.

> [T]he United States is a country, not a product, a news event or a movie, and its government and people need to explain themselves abroad in an in-depth manner to maintain and expand their influence in the international arena. *Even with global communications and "Americanization," other nations will continue to have their distinct cultures and ways of looking at reality; for our own national survival in an age of terror, we cannot afford to think that others will eventually become "like us" to the point where there is no need to persuade or communicate with them through public diplomacy.* [emphasis added][27]

This salutary acknowledgement of "distinct cultures and ways of looking at reality" still falls short of asking whether there might be merit in some of those other ways of looking at reality. In a nutshell, is the Muslim charge that the West is anti-Muslim true? And if it is true, should the West do something about it? Or do the Muslims just have to grit their teeth and endure this hostility in order to get those western goods, whether technological, ideological, or economic, that they find desirable?

Pronouncements by top government officials, like former CIA Director James Woolsey, who has embraced the notion that the War on Terror is World War IV—World War III was the Cold War—encourage Muslims to feel that they are collectively the target of American wrath:

> Clearly, the terror war is never going to go away until we change the face of the Middle East, which is what we are beginning to do in Iraq. That is a tall order. But it's not as tall an order as what we have already accomplished in the previous world wars.
>
> Change remains to be undertaken in that one part of the world that has historically not had democracy, which has reacted angrily against intrusions from the outside—the Arab Middle East.

Saddam Hussein, autocrats from the Saudi royal family and terrorists alike must realize that now, for the fourth time in 100 years,
America has been awakened. This country is on the march. We did-
n't choose this fight—the Baathist fascists, the Islamist Shia and the
Islamist Sunni did—but we're in it. And being on the march, there's
only one way we're going to be able to win it. It's the way we won
World War I, fighting for Wilson's 14 points. It is the way we won
World War II, fighting for Churchill and Roosevelt's Atlantic Charter. It is the way we won World War III, fighting for the noble ideas
best expressed by President Reagan but also very importantly at the
beginning by President Truman.

This war, like the world wars of the past, is not a war of us against
them. It is not a war between countries. It is a war of freedom against
tyranny.[28]

The distortions of history contained in these few paragraphs—
most sadly the exclusion from the roster of American stalwarts
against communism of Presidents Eisenhower, Kennedy, John-
son, Nixon, and Carter, all of whom confronted communist military expansion—are emblematic of the degree to which ideology
is coming to prevail over common sense in the American policy
community. Americans did not fight World War I for Wilson's
Fourteen Points. The war had already been over for two months
when that policy was enunciated. Nor did Americans fight World
War II for the Atlantic Charter. The pact between Roosevelt and
Churchill, signed four months before Pearl Harbor, made no mention of Japan or of America becoming a combatant nation. More
importantly, both the Fourteen Points and the Atlantic Charter
proclaimed, as the latter put it, "the right of all peoples to choose
the form of government under which they will live." As the course
of history unfolded, respect for this right took second place to imperialist ambition. Great Britain and France assumed control of
the Middle East after World War I, and the signatories to the
United Nations Declaration of 1942, which embodied the Atlantic
Charter, included imperialist nations like Great Britain, Belgium,

and the Netherlands that had no intention of freeing their colonies at war's end.

This historical failure of the imperialist countries to fulfill the principles for which the first two world wars were allegedly fought leads Woolsey to a phenomenally obtuse conclusion: "Change remains to be undertaken in that one part of the world that has historically not had democracy, which has reacted angrily against intrusions from the outside—the Arab Middle East." By "intrusions from the outside," can Woolsey be referring to anything other than imperialist occupation and manipulation? Does he really believe that it was wrong of the people of the Middle East to "react angrily" to these betrayals of wartime promises? One can only hope that his words were simply ill-considered, in the fashion of so many statements made by American leaders that deeply offend Middle Eastern and Muslim audiences.

Capping his apparent endorsement of imperialism, and seemingly blind to the hypocrisy it represents with respect to the ideals he claims to espouse, Woolsey proceeds to list our enemies in World War IV: on the one hand, "Saddam Hussein, autocrats from the Saudi royal family and terrorists;" on the other, "Baathist fascists, the Islamist Shia and the Islamist Sunni." Who has he left out? First, U.S.-supported governments like those of Algeria, Egypt, Tunisia, and Turkey that employ police state measures to suppress political participation by Muslim activists seeking access to the electoral system. Second, the "English-speaking, Western-educated intellectuals" already mentioned in 1957 as the favored interlocutors of American diplomats and catapulted into prominence—often after spending decades in the United States as émigrés—as the potential founding fathers of Middle Eastern democracy after the conquest of Iraq in 2003. No Muslim can be sure what Woolsey and like-minded officials mean when they use the word "Islamist," but it does not take a particularly skeptical mind to surmise that the United States is no more prepared today to tolerate an Islamic road to modernity than it was when Muslim revolutionaries deposed the tyrannical Shah of Iran in 1979.

For adumbrations of a more pluralistic and less rigid viewpoint, one can turn to a United Nations document entitled "Arab Human Development Report 2002." This report gained wide and deserved publicity for its frank assessment of conditions in an Arab world whose cultural and educational landscape it presents as unremittingly bleak and stagnant. It was authored by a group of Arab intellectuals, however, not by American officialdom, and its United Nations auspices further distance it from the world of American policy-making. Though unquestionably secular in tone, the report nevertheless exhibits an awareness that large segments of the Arab world look at politics and society through religious eyes, and an appreciation of the fact that this optic cannot be ignored. It begins with a blunt but moderately worded statement of the problem:

> There is a substantial lag between Arab countries and other regions in terms of participatory governance. . . . This freedom deficit undermines human development and is one of the most painful manifestations of lagging political development. While de jure acceptance of democracy and human rights is enshrined in constitutions, legal codes and government pronouncements, de facto implementation is often neglected and, in some cases, deliberately disregarded.
>
> In most cases, the governance pattern is characterized by a powerful executive branch that exerts significant control over all other branches of the state, being in some cases free from institutional checks and balances. Representative democracy is not always genuine and sometimes absent. Freedoms of expression and association are frequently curtailed. Obsolete norms of legitimacy prevail.[29]

The opening toward Islam comes in a section entitled "An Open Culture of Excellence":

> Culture and values are the soul of development. They provide its impetus, facilitate the means needed to further it, and substantially define people's vision of its purposes and ends. Culture and values are

instrumental in the sense that they help to shape people's daily hopes, fears, ambitions, attitudes and actions, but they are also formative because they mould people's ideals and inspire their dreams for a fulfilling life for themselves and future generations. There is some debate in Arab countries about whether culture and values promote or retard development. Ultimately, however, values are not the servants of development; they are its wellspring. . . .

Governments—Arab or otherwise—cannot decree their people's values; indeed, governments and their actions are partly formed by national cultures and values. . . .

Traditional culture and values, including traditional Arab culture and values, can be at odds with those of the globalizing world. Given rising global interdependence, the most viable response will be one of openness and constructive engagement whereby Arab countries both contribute to and benefit from globalization. The values of democracy also have a part to play in this process of resolving differences between cultural traditionalism and global modernity. Different people will have different preferences, some welcoming global influences, others resenting their pervasive impact. In a democratic framework, citizens can decide how to appraise and influence cultural changes, taking account of a diversity of views and striking a balance between individual liberty and popular preferences in the difficult choices involved.[30]

Half a century after Daniel Lerner helped embed modernization theory at the heart of Middle East studies, the two score Arab intellectuals who contributed to this study, some of them surely the sons and daughters of his "men-on-the-move" of 1950, announce clearly and politely that as "spokesmen" for their societies they do not concur with Lerner's bedrock assumption that "what the West is . . . the Middle East seeks to become." Under the discreet veil of "culture and values," Islam has regained a place at the negotiating table. The question is whether Lerner's conceit that "the Western model of modernization as a baseline is forced upon us . . . by the tacit assumptions and proclaimed goals which prevail among Middle East spokesmen" still survives in American educational and policy circles. It was one thing to aver in 1950 that the desires of the people of the Middle East—putatively to become just like us— should dictate the analyses of change carried out by American scholars. It is quite another to propose that if the voters in a Middle Eastern or Muslim country desire a government that will observe Muslim norms and values, Americans should look with equanimity upon that outcome.

## A Conversation

It may appear that my line of argument has gotten lost, but it's just been hiding. Let me flush it into the open. Before World War II, American missionaries in the Middle East looked for souls to save. They usually couldn't save them because local laws prohibited converting Muslims, but they could at least bestow some Christian love upon them, and seek to be loved in return.

After the war, the founders of Middle East Studies ignored recommendations that they focus on contemporary Islam and focused instead on Middle Easterners trying to act like westerners. There weren't a lot of these, just as there hadn't been a lot of converts, but the conviction was strong that those few would be pioneers in bringing western modernity to the region. In their heart of hearts, the founders believed, Middle Easterners—in fact, everyone in the nonwestern world—wanted their societies to be like those in the West.

The people we supported as agents of modernity became tyrants, their societies police states. A surer grasp of the political culture of Islam might have warned us of this, but we were infatuated with men on the move. Though we were disappointed when they did not act as our theorists had predicted, we did not give up on them.

The Iranian Revolution proved particularly trying. We loved the Shah, and he loved us in return. But he was a tyrant, and his subjects wanted a voice in government. Lacking a better understanding of Islam, we couldn't understand why so many Iranians thought that turbaned mullahs could lead them, much less design a demo-cratic government. After all, modernizers were supposed to be peo-ple just like us.

Then Osama bin Laden came along and confirmed the theories, at least in the reckoning of analysts who believe that he and his fol-lowers hate the modern world. But this left us with a confusing picture. Some religious activists seemed to want elections and some sort of integration into the modern world. Or did they? Others seemed to hate western civilization and yearn for theocra-cy? Or did they?

Islam, which the theorists had dismissed as a fading vestige of the past, became a source of puzzlement. Could we trust them? Could we like them? Could they like us? The aftermath of the sec-ond Gulf War proved a test. Ahmad Chelabi, a well-tailored, well-healed friend of the American administration, was the classic man on the move. But the Iraqis inexplicably didn't seem to care for him. The Shi'ite mullahs in Najaf, on the other hand, had thou-sands of enthusiastic followers. But we had no idea what they re-ally stood for. Again, our failure to comprehend the centuries-old dynamic of Islamic political theory clouded our vision.

The problem is vexing, but it is not new. At a conference on the twenty-first century held in Japan in 1993, a distinguished Colum-bia University colleague of unimpeachably liberal outlook was dis-cussing the 1992 Algerian coup that suspended parliamentary elec-tions, which the Islamic Salvation Front (FIS) had been sure to win. The coup had troubled him when it occurred, he said, but on reflection he had decided that stopping the election was better than allowing the men who assassinated Anwar Sadat to come to power. Pointing out that Algeria was not Egypt and that the FIS and the violent fringe group that carried out the assassination were unconnected did not dissuade him from his view. His unal-terable opinion was that terrorists acting in the name of Islam were indistinguishable from Muslim political parties seeking ac-cess to the electoral process.

Lumping religious terrorists and religious democrats together appeals to many Americans. But even people whose unfriendliness toward Islam is beyond doubt don't always seem sure. The WINEP *Special Policy Forum Report* cited above quotes Daniel Pipes: "The United States can promote a modern, moderate, good-neighborly version of Islam, but it cannot on its own ensure the ascendancy of such a vision. Only Muslims can do this." It sounds like we should be looking for *good* Muslims to love. Then he continues in a more characteristic vein: "There is no such thing as a moderate Islamist, for all Islamists share the same long-term goals; they differ only over means."[31]

Pipes' fellow panelist, independent scholar and former CIA analyst Graham Fuller, follows with a friendlier point of view:

> Islamism is not analogous to fascism or communism. Rather, it is a religious, political, and cultural framework that addresses the concerns of Muslims, serving as a more attractive alternative to past Arab ideological movements that failed to deliver what ordinary Muslims need. The Islamist phenomenon is a result of global trends toward modernization, a response to the problems and aspirations of the modern world. Islamism is part of the universal struggle to make sense of a troubling world, in this case using religion. . . . Democratization will be a long process . . . Muslim populations have been penned in for years, and when the gates open, it will be a rough ride. Islamists will win the first elections, but will they win the second? If Islamists do not deliver once in power, they will fail.[32]

The general American outlook on Islam pays little heed to quarrels among specialists, including those aired at clairvoyant think-tank conferences. Virtually all thoughtful Americans shudder at the idea of Islamists forming governments, even through free elections. But they are generally hazy on what the word "Islamist" actually means. Liberals shudder because of the illiberalism they see at the heart of Islamic movements. Conservatives shudder because of the anti-Americanism they see in those same movements. Both consider the separation of church and state sacrosanct, even though they know little about the relations between mosque and state in Muslim history.

The idea of a Muslim political party frightens most Americans, even though parties labeled Christian Democrat have formed governments in several European countries. Closer to home, many of those who want Islam out of politics support the political activities of Christian fundamentalist groups in the United States and/or Jewish religious parties in Israel. They sometimes deplore the specific policy prescriptions of Christian and Jewish political activists, but they invariably defend their right to stand for election.

Does acceptance of Christian and Jewish politics and rejection of Muslim politics have a credible rationale? Or is this split vision simply anti-Muslim prejudice? And what of the many Muslims who share the American distaste for Islamic politics? Calling them "men on the move" sounds antique. But is Daniel Pipes' vision of anti-Islamist Muslims who can construct an America-approved "modern, moderate, good-neighborly version of Islam" any different?

A conversation I had—somewhat reconstructed—with a male Moroccan graduate student at Columbia, is representative of stand-offs I've encountered in trying to assess Muslim attitudes:

> STUDENT: Professor, you've said that you consider the coup that prevented the FIS from winning the Algerian parliamentary elections a terrible mistake. But how do you respond to the oft-made claim that if they had won, it would have been a case of "one man, one vote, one time"? Moreover, wouldn't they have curtailed the freedom of Algerian women?
>
> PROFESSOR: Let's take the "one man, one vote, one time" charge first. It's obvious that in any country that is holding free elections, particularly if it is for the first time, there is no way of knowing whether the winners of the election will relinquish power when their term in office ends. Indeed, there are many cases of presidents and parties not leaving office. "One man, one vote, one

time" has been the sad story in a number of African and Latin American countries. In the Middle East, elections in Syria, Iraq, Tunisia, Egypt, and, for a long time, Turkey, have simply served to perpetuate the rule of single-party regimes. This is not solely a non-European problem. Think of Louis Napoleon, Adolf Hitler, and various post–World War II communist regimes in eastern Europe. Indeed, in American history there were people who feared that George Washington, like Mustafa Kemal Atatürk or Gamal Abdel Nasser, would never give up the presidency once he was elected. Yet no one ever bans the most egregious offenders, generals and heads of nationalist parties, from running for office. Why? Because it is assumed that the risk of an elected government subsequently subverting the electoral process is a risk worth taking in the interest of establishing democracy. So why are Islamist parties singled out for suspicion? There is no historical precedent for ascribing such malign motives to them.

STUDENT: But don't they say that they want to create an Islamic republic and monopolize power?

PROFESSOR: Sometimes they do, but various communist parties have similarly aspired to create fully communist regimes. In some countries, this aspiration has led to communists being barred from running for office. But in some countries where communist parties have won elections, such as India, they have neither created totalitarian regimes nor refused to relinquish office when defeated in subsequent elections. In the United States we do not bar communists from running for office, but we make a sworn commitment to uphold the Constitution a condition for serving.

STUDENT: But take the case of Iran. Parties that do not support an Islamic republic are excluded from elections, and candidates for office have to be approved by a committee of mullahs. If the FIS had been elected, they would have emulated the Iranians and created an Islamic republic in Algeria.

PROFESSOR: What you say about Iran is certainly true, but the Islamic Republic of Iran did not come into being through the election of an Islamist party running against non-Islamist opponents.

It came into being through a revolution, followed by a constitutional referendum. We have to distinguish between ordinary elections and constitutional referenda. If the FIS had won in Algeria, it's altogether possible that it would have sought the establishment of an Islamic republic. Two possible strategies come to mind: a military coup, which would have been hard to pull off given the power of secularists in the military command; or promulgation of a new constitution, which was possible but would have required a massive parliamentary majority. Possibly the majority of the Algerian people would subsequently have voted for an Islamic republic; but if they had, and if the military had permitted that vote to be implemented, on what democratic basis can you or I say that the Algerians should have been denied the opportunity to choose that form of government?

STUDENT: On the basis that an Islamic republic would have denied a voice in government to minority views and would have oppressed the people—and women in particular—by forcing them to abide by religious rules.

PROFESSOR: What you say is possible, but it is not necessarily certain. An Islamic republic can take different constitutional forms. In Iran, the constitution guarantees parliamentary representation for certain religious minorities, but permits oppression of Baha'ism, which is not recognized as an independent religion. Women vote and run for office, but they suffer restrictions on their public behavior. These are serious imperfections and ones that call to mind the age-old fear of an electoral majority suppressing minority rights. But this is not solely a problem with Islam. The authors of the American constitution, for example, unlike the major Islamist parties throughout the Muslim world today, made no provision for women voting and did not prohibit African slavery. Their democracy was not for everyone. Moreover, one has to wonder whether in 1790 a royalist would have been able to run for election in the United States on a platform of returning the country to British rule. In more recent times, it is evident that Turkey has devoted as much effort to denying voters the choice of religious electoral candidates as Iran has expended on excluding royalists and secularists from standing as candidates.

STUDENT: That may be true, but clearly there is a difference. The Turkish policy arises from a desire to separate church and state, a principle that is at the heart of democracy, while the Iranians are imposing religion on everyone whether they want it or not.

PROFESSOR: Separation of church and state has assuredly become an important principle of European and American democracy. But it was not originally a cornerstone of the U.S. Constitution. The bar on legislation establishing an official religion appears in the First Amendment, adopted two years after the Constitution, and it applied only to the federal government until the Fourteenth Amendment in 1868 extended the principles of the Bill of Rights to the states. As the federally recognized territorial governor of Utah between 1850 and 1857, Brigham Young certainly did not change his views on the dominant role of religion in public affairs. As for how Americans have understood the "established religion" clause, interpretation has changed over the past two centuries as the United States has become more secular. Yet the storm of protest that met a Federal Court's removal of the words "under God" from the Pledge of Allegiance attests to the continuing objections of many people of faith to the most rigorous efforts to enforce separation.

STUDENT: We're not talking here about the Pledge of Allegiance or prayer in schools. Islam is not like Catholicism and Protestantism in the United States. Islam has dominated the outlook of people in the Middle East for so many centuries that permitting it to play a role in government will inevitably lead to the imposition of a religious state and the end of democracy.

PROFESSOR: The same might have been said of the hold eighteenth-century Christianity had on popular sentiment at the dawn of democratic government in Europe and America. The democrats of the French Revolution tried to eliminate the influence of the church in all aspects of society. Their anticlerical approach became a model for the Europeanizing Middle Eastern governments of the nineteenth and twentieth centuries. By contrast, American democrats erected a firewall between church and state, but retained the tradition of tax exemptions for religious bodies and did nothing to curtail their social and educational activities. Following a third path, English democrats—so long as they weren't Catholic—saw nothing wrong with having the Church of England as the established faith of the land, this being the form of church-state relationship that the American Bill of Rights explicitly prohibited. In Israel, finally, religious political parties wield their influence in the Knesset to gain substantial government benefits for their pious followers. Historically, therefore, American-style separation of church and state has not always gone hand in hand with democracy. In a general way, however, attachment to religion as a basis for government does seem to diminish with prolonged exposure to democratic practices. Secularists may reasonably hope that the institution of democratic regimes in Muslim countries will lead in time to a largely secular political culture; but it is naïve to think, as the Bolsheviks did, that one can quickly cut people off from their religious roots by government decree, particularly if the government issuing the decrees has to face elections.

STUDENT: What you are saying, then, is that people who call for democracy have to accept whatever comes along, even if it forces secular citizens into exile and compels women to wear veils. Religious tyranny is okay so long as it is supported by a majority of the voters, many of whom are poorly educated and subject to the guidance of religious leaders and demagogues.

PROFESSOR: Things need not be quite so horrendous as you describe. Every democratic regime has a written or unwritten constitution, and constitutions set limits for government activity. Officials take oaths to uphold the constitution, and there is usually a supreme judicial authority that decides what is or is not in accord with the constitution. The crafting of a constitution is a key step in the transition from an authoritarian state to a democratic state. Whether devising an Islamic republic, a secular republic, a pluralist republic, or a constitutional monarchy, the framers of a constitution have to decide where to lodge the ultimate sanctions of legitimacy. A monarchy may make the ruler the ultimate arbiter, but many constitutional monarchs wield no power. An Islamic republic may insert into the governing structure a committee or individual—in Iran's case both—charged with ensuring that government actions do not violate religious strictures. But that is not the case in Pakistan, which calls itself an Islamic republic but looks constitutionally to a strong presidency and a supreme court for ultimate legitimacy. In other models—notably Turkey and Algeria—the army guarantees the constitution, even if the structure of that guarantee is not explicitly spelled out.

STUDENT: But constitutions can change—and will change if Islamists come to power.

PROFESSOR: They can indeed, but changes are usually difficult to transact and require popular votes. I don't imagine that any of the framers of the U.S. constitution imagined a day would come when a supermajority of the states would agree to grant the vote to women. A constitutional prohibition on the transportation, sale, and manufacture of intoxicating liquors would equally have astounded them. The former amendment, which passed in 1920, we now take to be a cornerstone of American democracy. The latter, which passed in 1919, now strikes us as a Taliban-like anomaly driven by Protestant fanaticism. Constitutions cannot protect a people absolutely from excesses endorsed by the majority of the electorate, but they can make the process of instituting such excesses slow and difficult, thus forcing the voters to think two and three times about whether they really want a particular change.

STUDENT: I notice that you've skirted the question of the oppression of women. They are half the population. Don't you think that it is an absolute moral wrong to hobble them with civil disabilities?

PROFESSOR: Yes I do. I cannot imagine any constitution written in this day and age being deemed democratic if it denied women the vote or sanctioned slavery. For that reason, my optimism with regard to the potential of Muslim political activism does not extend to movements calling for an Islamic autocracy unconstrained by electoral institutions, whether the ruler is called an emir, a king, or a caliph. Most Muslim political movements endorse elections and call for women's suffrage. Some, like the Taliban and the zealots clustered around Osama bin Laden, do not. Giving women the vote is not the same thing as freeing them from social disabilities, however. Social practices do not change overnight, nor is adherence to European or American customs the best way of assessing the status of women. From my perspective, the right to vote, access to jobs, and fairness in marriage, divorce, and child custody seem of a higher priority than regulations on costume. Some women I know disagree and tell me that I fail to understand the symbolic character of dress restrictions. Not being immersed in a Muslim cultural milieu, I will leave these judgments to people who are. But it does strike me as a peculiarity of American self-righteousness that after a century of missionary striving to persuade women in non-European lands to cover their bosoms, a morbid fascination that continues to the present day in local prohibitions on topless beaches, Americans now devote equivalent zeal to urging Muslim women to exhibit their hair.

STUDENT: I'm amazed that you would trivialize such an important issue this way.

PROFESSOR: I don't mean to trivialize it. I was simply observing that American views on gender matters in the Muslim world are less important than the views of Muslims. Given access to elections, Muslim women will fight their own battles.

STUDENT: That may well be; but all in all, I remain unconvinced by your many arguments. I wouldn't say that I never want to live in an Islamist state, or that Islamists should be prevented from coming to power. But I do think there should be an overseeing authority—the military or maybe the judiciary—that will step in if the Islamists try to do away with elections, fundamentally change the constitution, or introduce measures opposed by much of the population.

I have been involved in variants of this conversation hundreds of times, but I don't believe I have ever thoroughly convinced my interlocutor. Distrust of political Islam runs very deep. Since I believe quite firmly in the soundness of my position, its weakness as a platform for debate concerns me.

Political events receive dramatically different evaluations as soon as Islam is involved. If Mohammed Reza Shah Pahlavi had emerged the victor in his confrontation with Ayatollah Khomeini in 1979, he might have guided a transition to a constitutional monarchy and instituted electoral reforms more or less identical to those that exist today, but with himself taking the place of the Governing Jurist (*Vali Faqih*), and a council of royal nominees taking the place of the mullah-dominated Council of Guardians. If this had happened, Iran would unquestionably be considered today a progressive and democratic country—even if, as a sop to clerical opposition, the Shah had put strictures on women's dress, spoken harshly of the United States and Israel, sought nuclear weapons capability, and scared his neighbors. On the other side of the coin, even moderate, electable, and politically savvy Islamists like Turkey's Recep Erdogan give hives to allergy-prone Islamophobes. Daniel Pipes, for example, ventures the opinion that, "The Justice and Development Party in Turkey is very different from the Taliban in its means, but not so different in its ends. If the party gained full control over Turkey, it could be as dangerous as the Taliban were in Afghanistan."[33]

Until there is a fundamental reconsideration of what Islam has meant as a political force for the past millennium and a half, and of the long-term sibling relationship between Islam and the West, the word Islam will continue to sound to western ears like a rattlesnake's rattle. A half-century of scholarly effort, following a full century of missionary attempts, to find or imagine Muslims Americans can love provides a weak foundation for the sort of reappraisal that is needed. But without a reappraisal, the future of American relations with the Muslim world will be thorny and unpredictable, haunted by dashed hopes and missed opportunities.

*The voices that will enunciate the pivotal ideas for the next great phase of Islamic history have probably not been heard yet.*

CHAPTER 4

# The Edge of the Future

ISLAM IS IMMERSED in a crisis of authority. From coed swimming and playing rock music to condemning Salman Rushdie and declaring a jihad against Jews and Crusaders, there are several positions on every question. If each position matched up with a particular authority, believers could make their choices. But it is no longer clear what constitutes an authority. The imam of the local mosque is the last word for many, but others follow the advice they glean from pamphlets, magazines, radio preachers, and Internet sites. For everyone who heeds the prescriptions of a government appointed dignitary, there is someone else who considers all dignitaries sellouts to the regime. Group gurus tell their followers what to think while noted intellectuals cast aspersions on all groups and sects.

Resolving this crisis of authority will take several generations. The history of religious fragmentation and divisiveness in the Christian West holds come clues to how things might evolve in the sibling faith community of Islam, but analogy has limits. Thirty years of thinking that Islam no longer counted for much, followed by twenty years of borderline hysteria about Islam as a looming threat, have prepared America poorly for looking dispassionately into the future of Islamo-Christian civilization.

A Muslim tradition holds that with every new century there comes a "renewer" (*mujaddid*), literally, a person whose mission it is to make Muslim religious life new. The renewer's role differs from that of the messiah *(mahdi)*, who comes only at the end of the world. The tradition of the renewer testifies to an ingrained Muslim confidence in the capacity of their faith to restore itself after periods of disunity or flagging spirit and to adapt to the challenges that the passage of centuries inevitably brings. Typically, no one agrees on who the renewer of a given century is until long after that individual's death—if then.

Some western scholars seem to believe that a professional career devoted to thinking about Islamic matters gives them the insight to recognize the renewer. A few may even dream of penning something of unutterable brilliance under a Muslim *nom de plume* and claiming the title for themselves. The British poet and traveler Wilfred Scawen Blunt may have thought he had spotted the renewer when he wrote *The Future of Islam* about the modernist thoughts of the Egyptian Muhammad Abduh. The year of publication was 1882, the very cusp of the Muslim fourteenth century, which began the following year. Traditionally, the beginning of a new century is a ripe time for the renewer to appear. Of more relevance to present-day matters, the turn of the fifteenth century in 1980—the Muslim lunar century is three years shorter than the solar century—brought with it not only the Islamic revolution in Iran but an enhanced feeling among Muslims and non-Muslims alike that something new and titanic was brewing. Since then, scores of authors have argued that Islam is in need of a Reformation, or more specifically, a Martin Luther, the Christian renewer *par excellence*.

The scholarly community has organized its search for renewers, redeemers, and messiahs with Cartesian finesse. Over the last two decades, conference papers and learned articles devoted to observing the contemporary Muslim religious scene and dividing the observed phenomena into analytical categories have multiplied like mushrooms on a dead log. Devising categories is second nature to academics. Authors usually feel free to construct their own typologies, classifying individual thinkers and movements as modernist, fundamentalist, jihadist, conservative, radical, moderate, Islamist, traditional, activist, quietist, rationalist, obscurantist, liberal, democratic, totalitarian . . . the list goes on. Since categories are indeed analytically useful, these efforts are not to be denigrated. Yet the Muslims subjected to classification seldom employ such categories in talking about themselves. Muslims who seek to lead their brothers and sisters into a better realization of their common faith more often speak in inclusive terms, leaving the reality of the proposed categories in limbo.

I will seek here neither to identify the renewer nor to classify Muslim thinkers and movements. Despite the urgency of Islam's crisis of authority, I see no reason to think that it will be resolved during my lifetime. Socioreligious developments tend to play out over decades and centuries because they involve a succession of generations becoming socialized to new religious expectations and conditions. Many of my students have heard me divide all of Islamic history into four-hundred-year segments: 600–1000, the initial era of conversion to Islam; 1000–1400, the era of conflict within Islam over what sorts of religious understandings should predominate in different Muslim communities; 1400–1800, the era of resistance to Christian expansion and of stable states built on societies that had resolved the problem of competing understandings; and 1800–2200, the era of the destruction of various Muslim social syntheses in the course of confrontation with the West, and of the creation of new socioreligious syntheses appropriate to the modern world. Ending this admittedly simplistic and half-facetious periodization at a point two centuries in the future is supposed to teach the lesson that a resolution of the crisis facing the Muslim world, and facing the West in its relations with the

Muslim world, may not be found in the next ten or twenty years, much less in the remaining years of the Bush administration. *The voices that will enunciate the pivotal ideas for the next great phase of Islamic history have probably not have been heard yet.*

As a non-Muslim, I do not feel comfortable surveying the multitude of tendencies and ideas currently competing for attention and highlighting those I find attractive and those I find repellent. But I do have biases. I favor articulations of Islam that include commitments to participatory government; I deplore articulations that advocate terrorism.

These biases do not represent any claim to clairvoyance in predicting how hundreds of millions of Muslims will choose to live their lives in the course of the twenty-first century, but I have never agreed with historian colleagues who shun envisioning the future. I think historians are at least as well prepared to think about the future as political scientists and sociologists. Better, in fact. The historical profession trains its practitioners to cobble together from fragmentary remains credible representations of times long past. The future shares with the distant past the feature of being outside contemporary experience. So why should the craftsmanship of the historian not work as well in putting together bits and pieces of evidence to project a plausible picture of things to come? I will divide my predictions into two categories, the edge, and the future.

## The Edge

My book *Islam: The View from the Edge,* published in 1994,[1] dealt for the most part with medieval Islam. But in it I advanced an approach to Islamic history that applies today. I focused on the experiences of people living in what I called "edge" situations, by which I meant situations where people were in the process of becoming Muslim through conversion, or of reconnecting to their religious roots through some sort of spiritual renewal. I called such social situations the "edge" of Islam for three reasons. First,

I wanted to distinguish between people in these situations and people living in the "center," a term I used to designate what historians conventionally consider the political and religious core of Muslim history: the caliphate and its successor states; the post-Mongol empires of the Ottomans, Safavids, and Mughals; the development of Islamic law; and the intellectual issues arising from the medieval confrontation with Aristotelian ideas. Secondly, I wanted to avoid the words "periphery" and "margin" because readers often understand them in purely geographical terms and instinctively consider the "center" more important. Thirdly, terms like "edgy" and "cutting edge" fit with my contention that the edge in Islam, rather than the center, has been where new things happen. Alas, a number of reviewers took my "edge" to be synonymous with geographical periphery, and even with provincial peculiarity. So I need to restate my argument.

In the absence of an ecclesiastical hierarchy, narratives of Islamic history put political institutions at the center of the story: first the caliphate and then a plethora of successor states, each with its judges, jurisconsults, and market inspectors as prescribed by the shari'a. Nevertheless, these political institutions generally lacked an extensive capacity for religious guidance. From the death of the Prophet onward, Muslims who wanted to know what was expected of them religiously did not look to the government. They followed instead the practices of their local community, as transmitted from generation to generation in written or oral form. Alternatively, they sought pastoral instruction from religious scholars and saintly individuals. Sometimes these were government officials, but usually not. In most times and places, the prevailing political institutions had little interest in or control over these sources of guidance.

Like people of all faiths, Muslims find important elements of identity and solace in observing as adults the practices they first encounter as children. Local custom does not offer such clear guidance, however, for people who are considering a change in their religious identity either by embracing a different variant of their ancestral faith; or by converting to a different religion. Nor does customary practice help people who think their community is too little involved with religion and who seek a more intensive religious experience; or the other direction, people who desire a more or less nonreligious way of life. All of these manifestations of the edge raise questions about how to behave and what to believe.

Edge situations, which have parallels in other religions, have been unusually creative in the history of Islam because answering questions raised by prospective converts to Islam, and by Muslims in spiritual quandary, exposes underlying ambiguities about the sources of spiritual authority. Muslims committed to the beliefs and practices of the center have few uncertainties in this area. The Quran; the hadith, or collected accounts of the words and deeds of Muhammad; the shari'a; and the consensus of learned Muslims on spiritual matters make it clear to them what it means to be a Muslim. But Islam's edges have often lacked such clarity, sometimes because of confrontation with local non-Muslim traditions, and sometimes because of the preaching of assertive individuals whose views differ from those of the center.

Zones of intercultural confrontation and unconventional preaching by charismatic individuals pose problems for all religions, of course, but formalized ecclesiastical structures usually suffice to minimize them. Absent such ecclesiastical structures, problems arise. Who is authorized to answer the questions posed by believers? Does the notion of "authorized response" mean much in edge contexts? What determines the legitimacy of charismatic preachers?

In drawing attention to the edge in Islam, I make no claim that the edge distinguishes Islam from other religions. I want, rather, to highlight the comparative potency of developments on the edge in conditions of weakly institutionalized religious authority. The center in Islam has a frequently expressed horror of innovation (*bid'a*) in matters of faith and practice. This position buttresses the widespread impression that Islam is an unchanging religion. The vitality of Islam's edge communities has developed in the face of this rhetorical abhorrence and given rise to remarkable diversity under the name of Islam. Confrontation between the conservative center and the creative edge will surely continue in the future as the current crisis of authority in Islam plays itself out.

Diversity exists in every religious tradition, but diversity has been particularly pronounced in Islam. This does not mean, however, that individual Muslims necessarily consider their faith to be marked by great diversity. To the contrary, uncertainty about what is authoritative can foster a tenacious adherence to practices and beliefs that specific communities consider to be the truest version of Islam. When there is no church acting as guardian of the faith, after all, the duty falls to the individual believer.

In the past, lack of contact between the Islam of the law courts and seminaries and edge communities in various regions resulted in some communities becoming strongly devoted to interpretations of Islam that differed a great deal from the legalistic norm. Some heartfelt expressions of Muslim faith even sound scandalous to other Muslims when they first hear of them. Examples may be found in many areas and periods, but two extreme illustrations from India and Indonesia will illustrate the point.

In the northern Indian state of Bihar in 1545, Mir Sayyid Rajgiri, known as Manjhan, composed a long poetic romance he entitled *Madhumalati*. Manjhan belonged to the Shattari Sufi brotherhood, an unquestionably Muslim devotional group. His tale of love treats metaphorically the Sufi's love of God. The poem begins:

> God, giver of love, the treasure-house of joy
> Creator of the two worlds in the one sound Om,
> my mind has no light worthy of you,
> with which to sing your praise, O Lord!
> King of the three worlds and the four ages,
> the world glorifies you from beginning to end . . .

Listen now while I tell of the man:
separated from him, the Maker became manifest.
When the Lord took on flesh, he entered creation.
The entire universe is of His Essence.
His radiance shone through all things.

This lamp of creation was named Muhammad!
For him, the Deity fashioned the universe,
and love's trumpet sounded in the triple worlds.
His name is Muhammad, king of three worlds.
He was the inspiration for creation.[2]

Anyone familiar with Hinduism will immediately recognize many of the religious doctrines contained in these lines. The cosmically creative syllable Om, the three worlds and four ages, and the presentation of Muhammad as a divine incarnation, correspond directly to Hindu doctrines and have no resemblance at all to most other versions of Islam. Evidently the Muslim faith community of northeastern India included many people who thought of themselves as Muslims but still retained their previous beliefs.[3] This was Islam on the edge: passionate, creative, adaptive, and attractive.

The Gayo highlands district of northern Sumatra in Indonesia affords a second example. As portrayed in a penetrating study by anthropologist John R. Bowen,[4] a local ritual specialist known as the Lord of the Fields bears the burden of negotiating a good harvest with the spirits, ancestors, and pests that affect the growing rice plants. The educated Muslim elite, the ulama, deplore the Lord of the Fields' rituals, but they do not openly contest them. For his part, the Lord of the Fields aligns his rituals with Islam, reciting "Qur'anic verses," which are actually spells in the local Achehnese language, that begin with the Arabic formula "In the name of God." He explains the spiritual connection between rice and Islam by means of the following myth:

The prophet Adam and Eve had a child, Tuan [Lady] Fatima. They lived on leaves from trees and rarely had enough to eat. Tuan Fatima wanted to marry the prophet Muhammad. She talked to him but without touching him, without intercourse—there was a barrier between them; he had seen her but not yet married her. But merely from that contact there was a spark between them, and she became pregnant by him without intercourse. She had a daughter, Maimunah.

God sent word to Muhammad by way of an angel that he should cut the child's throat, cut her up into little pieces (as you would a jackfruit—but you needn't write that down), and scatter the pieces into the field. The pieces became rice seeds, and grew to become rice plants.

Adam asked Fatima where her daughter was. She answered that she did not know. Adam replied that Muhammad was the father of the child and that he had scattered the child into the field. Eve said that Fatima must have slept with Muhammad and must marry him. Fatima swore that she had not, that they had only spoken, with a barrier between them. Then Jibra'il, Mika'il, Abu Bakr, Uthman, 'Ali, and Shi'a all came down from the sky and married the two (Shi'a sits to the immediate left of God). Muhammad did not refuse.

Muhammad then took Fatima into the field and showed her the rice and Fatima called out her child's name. Maimunah then answered, saying: "Don't look for me anymore, mother; I have become your means of life."[5]

For most Muslims, this story is horrifying. Nothing is so strongly and explicitly condemned in the Quran as female infanticide, and the intimation of incest in the relationship between Fatima and Muhammad, who was historically her father, is morally appalling. One might also sense Christian, Hindu, and Buddhist influences in the story. The sacrifice of the child born of a virgin for the well being of the whole community sounds Christian. The descent of heavenly beings sounds Hindu or Buddhist, even though the first two of them bear the Arabic names of angels; the next three commemorate early caliphs, including Fatima's historical husband, Ali; and the last is a personification of the Shi'ite sect of Islam, which has few practitioners in Indonesia. Yet despite this mixing of religions, there is no question that the Lord of the Fields who narrated the myth to Bowen considered himself a Muslim, and was so considered by the farmers in his community.

I have chosen for these examples versions of Islam that depart dramatically from what most people, both Muslims and non-Muslims, consider Islam to stand for. Such radical departures from an imagined norm sound strange, if not outright offensive, to most Muslims. But they are not uncommon in certain parts of the Muslim world, and they were probably even more common prior to the spread of literacy and modern media. What they share, in most cases, is a development on the edge. In the case of northeast India in the sixteenth century and Sumatra more recently, the edge was also part of a geographical periphery, but this does not mean that divergent articulations of Islam cannot be found in the old Islamic heartland of the Middle East and North Africa. The Druze of Lebanon, the Alevis of Turkey, and the Alawis of Syria, for example, profess doctrines that many neighboring Muslims find unconventional. These happen to date from medieval times when edge communities, consisting mostly of new converts, formed in many parts of the geographical heartland. In more recent times, the nineteenth-century movements of the Baha'is in Iran and Ahmadis in Pakistan showed great vigor and a capacity to attract both converts to Islam and Muslims looking for new spiritual experiences. Both movements carried out successful missionary operations in non-Muslim lands such as the United States, where the Ahmadis met success among African-Americans and the Baha'is among white Americans.

Today there is a strong impetus in many parts of the Muslim world to suppress divergent local beliefs and win people to more conventional interpretations of Islam. Missionary (*da'wa*) efforts based in Saudi Arabia are particularly active. This does not mean, however, that unconventional practices and beliefs on the edge are necessarily doomed to be overwritten by stronger influences from the center. Several major developments that are now considered integral to the Islam of the center originally formed on the edge. Collecting the sayings of Muhammad, for example, flourished in Iran at a time when conversion to Islam was at a particularly dynamic point. All six of the collections that Sunni Muslims eventually canonized as the truest expressions of their prophet's faith and practice were compiled in Iran during the ninth century. A second example: Religious seminaries (*madrasas*) first appeared in the tenth century far to the northeast of the Arab heartland in the frontier zone that today separates Iran from Afghanistan and Turkmenistan. Some historians suspect a Buddhist institutional origin. Only after two centuries of local development on the edge did these institutions spread throughout much of the Muslim world and standardize both Sunni and Shi'ite education. Sufi brotherhoods afford a third example of creation on the edge feeding back into the center. Some of the most successful brotherhoods, such as the Mevleviya and the Bektashiya, originated in what is today Turkey during the period of religious ferment that followed the collapse of Byzantine Christian power there in 1071. Other popular brotherhoods that enjoyed widespread success arose in other edge situations, such as the mountains of central Afghanistan (the Chishtiya), among the mixed Arab-Berber populations of North Africa (the Tijaniya), and, as we have seen, in northeast India (the Shattariya).

Developments like these demonstrate that Muslim communities that are remote from what appears at any point in time to be Islam's center have shown remarkable dynamism, creativity, and adaptability. They further demonstrate that some of edge developments have subsequently become incorporated into the Islam of the center. A search for parallels in other religions would most likely lead to the history of sects and denominations. However, the flexibility that has characterized Islam historically discourages such an approach. Though divisions within Islam have from time to time acquired names and become formalized, the flow of ideas, practices, and beliefs within and among communities discourages efforts to discover precise and permanent intrafaith boundaries. The annual mingling of hundreds of thousands of Muslims of every variety of belief during the pilgrimage to Mecca symbolizes this fluidity.

Looking at contemporary circumstances, it is evident that Muslims are living in a time of many edges. Observers agree that Islam is growing rapidly through conversion, the most common locus of edge developments. This is occurring in interfaith frontier zones in the Western Hemisphere, Africa, and Europe rather than in the old geographical heartland of the faith. Just as importantly, Muslims in many regions are actively seeking to intensify their religious lives while others are trying to adjust their religious observances to a secular society. Edges of this sort exist in all parts of the Muslim world. In the old Muslim heartland, they are often accompanied by an attitude of self-help and social responsibility framed against the failure of nationalist anticlerical government. In the re-Islamizing post-Soviet republics, violence in the name of Islam garners the headlines while the quiet multiplication of mosques and schools begins to reverse two generations of official atheism. In European and American diaspora communities, Muslims discuss ways of coping with governments and societies that they increasingly see as unfriendly, if not actually hostile.

Given the history of edge phenomena in Islam, what should be expected today is the appearance of myriad diverse movements addressing the spiritual and social needs of specific groups of believers. What should further be expected is that conservative voices from the center—including both governments in majority Muslim countries and the marginalized traditional ulama—will weigh less in the future spiritual balance than some of the new expressions of Islam on the edge. Overviews of Muslim religious activity worldwide, whether by Muslims or non-Muslims (and among non-Muslims, whether by people gazing about in fear and hatred, or by others of more friendly disposition) support both of these expectations. Thus in all likelihood, tomorrow's center will develop on today's edge.

## The Future

Two things separate the edges of today from those of the past: the speed and ease of communication, and the disappearance or devaluation of institutions conferring credentials of religious authority. For the first time in history, Muslims from every land and condition—a preacher in Harlem, a terrorist in Mombasa, a political party leader in Kuala Lumpur, a feminist in Marrakesh—can access a worldwide audience as easily as traditional authorities like a Shaikh al-Azhar in Cairo, an ayatollah in Najaf, or a royally appointed mufti in Riyadh. Moreover, the devaluation of the old authorities by the modernizing regimes of the nineteenth and twentieth centuries, and the creation of mass youth literacy by these same governments, have led many Muslims on the edge to believe that they are free to choose whatever brand of Islam best suits their circumstances. Of course, Muslims of conservative bent still declare that Islam can only be authoritatively defined by officially empowered qadis, muftis, and ulama. But others contend that Islam is whatever they and their friends believe it to be on the basis of the teachings of the person whose writings, audiotapes, and videotapes they find most convincing.

The edge perspective on Islamic history indicates that the resolution of this crisis of authority will depend less on ideas than on institutions, and in particular on institutions that convince large segments of the Muslim community that a semblance of spiritual order has returned. A free market in religious belief is a mixed blessing, at best, at a time when war clouds are gathering, voices of religious hatred are gaining a hearing, and millions of Muslims are struggling to raise their families in countries that are sinking deeper and deeper into poverty and disorder. People who turn to religion for spiritual and moral sustenance, and for the comfort that comes from living within a caring and supportive religious community, prefer assurance to debate in the delineation of the right path. At the present moment, the paths are many, but assurance based on recognized authority is in short supply.

Again, I claim no clairvoyance about the path or paths that will lead the world's Muslims through the coming century. I am inclined to doubt, in fact, that the options currently before them include the ones that will prove the most fruitful in the long run. Instead of describing religious ideas and interpretations, therefore, I will devote the remainder of this discussion to the challenges facing new experiments in institutionalizing authority.

Though some students of the Islamic Republic of Iran consider its effort to combine religion with government an abject failure, and others consider it a fascinating experiment in implementing democracy in an Islamic religious state, most would agree that its constitution writers boldly came to grips with the problem of institutionalizing religious authority, in the person of the "governing religious jurist" (*vali faqih*). To date, no parallel has emerged in the Sunni world. There are doubtless many reasons for the Shi'ite ulama's comparative success in this endeavor, but looking toward the future, one reason that is particularly suggestive concerns a five-century debate between two factions of those ulama, the Akhbaris and the Usulis.

The Akhbari school of thought maintained that all authoritative Shi'ite knowledge could be found in voluminous texts from earlier times. "Akhbar," the modern Arabic word for "news," refers to those texts, which were mostly composed when Shi'ism was out of power and strongly marked by political quietism. This school held that the ulama should remain aloof from political affairs until the return of the Hidden Imam. The opposing Usuli school of thought took its name from the Arabic phrase *usul al-din*, meaning "roots of the faith." It asserted that by virtue of their understanding of fundamental religious principles, the *usul*, the top ulama were qualified to pronounce binding judgments on contemporary problems because they were more likely than any government official to know how the Hidden Imam might judge things. In Usuli thinking, there was no need to be bound by bygone texts. A truly learned scholar was fully qualified to exercise his independent, but informed, judgment, or *ijtihad*.

The debate developed from the sixteenth century onward against the background of the rise and fall of the Safavids, the most powerful Shi'ite dynasty ever to rule in Iran. The crux of the matter was whether in the absence of the Hidden Imam, the shah's government was legitimate enough to declare jihad and perform other religiously authorized functions. The Usulis supported government authority, and then went farther and claimed that they themselves knew better how to rule.

By the end of the eighteenth century, the Usulis had won the argument and assumed control of the major Shi'ite seminaries. The most highly esteemed ulama were judged by their fellows to be *mujtahids*, or scholars qualified to exercise independent judgment. Ordinary believers were expected to conform their beliefs and actions to the guidance of a single living mujtahid, a "reference point of emulation" (*marja' al-taqlid*), and to shift their allegiance to another living mujtahid upon the death of their first. These developments paved the way for Ayatollah Khomeini and others to create a new form of government on their own initiative and to command the respect of the majority of the population in doing so.

The religiously questionable legitimacy of the Safavid shahs anticipated by three centuries similar problems that confronted Sunni societies in the nineteenth century. In India, Algeria, sub-Saharan Africa, and the Muslim territories absorbed into the Russian empire, Sunni ulama saw their political institutions fall prey to aggressive Christian imperialism. Meanwhile, in Egypt and the Ottoman Empire, Westernizing regimes undermined the ulama in unsuccessful efforts to stave off imperialism. In the face of what they saw as an assault on their religion and their professional status, some Sunni ulama concluded that what Islam needed was a renewal of the seldom exercised—some thought banned—practice of *ijtihad*, the same practice that their Usuli Shi'ite counterparts had already resuscitated.

Unlike the Shi'ites, however, they did not reach a consensus on what would qualify a person as a *mujtahid*, nor did they figure out whether or how ordinary Muslims could be made to follow new independent judgments. The problem that the Usuli Shi'ites, with a long head start and a smaller and more concentrated body of followers, had solved by recognizing a few "reference points of emulation," and requiring ordinary believers to follow their rulings, remains unsolved in Sunni Islam to the present day. The widespread

loss of trust in the old authorities and their institutions has resulted in hundreds of acts of *ijtihad* embodied in *fatwas* (legal opinions) or less formal declarations, but no way of telling which of
them should be followed. Moreover, many of these new pronouncements have been made by individuals whose religious credentials would have been laughed at in the eighteenth century.
Thus ordinary Muslims are understandably uncertain as to where
true authority lies.

My contention that institutional developments will prove more
important than doctrines, innovative or otherwise, over the coming
decades is rooted in this crisis situation. Judging from history,
Sunni Islam will surely not continue indefinitely under the current
radical breakdown in its structure of authority. Nor is it clear that
the Usuli Shi'ite solution will prove sufficiently adaptable to sur-
vive. The issues are clear for both Sunnis and Shi'ites: New ways
must be found to credential and empower religious authorities. Ordinary believers must be persuaded to follow the decisions of those
authorities. And people with inadequate credentials must be accorded a lesser standing. Getting ordinary Muslims to accept a new
authority structure, however, will depend on whether that structure
is responsive to today's moral, political, and social problems.

While the religious edges of our time seem certain to generate a
number of creative ways of resolving Islam's crisis of authority, Islamic history cannot predict what form these will take. In the past,
the developers of authoritative religious institutions assumed that
political boundaries were irrelevant. Schools of legal interpretation, the practice of collecting and winnowing the traditions of
Muhammad, the establishment of seminaries, and the formation
of Sufi brotherhoods all crossed political boundaries. Rulers enjoyed the right to appoint judges to law courts located within their
realms, but the law itself reflected the thoughts and decisions of
legal scholars from many lands and was beyond state control. Similarly, while rulers and their families often patronized seminaries
and Sufi sheikhs, they could not dictate the curricula of the
schools or the teachings of the sheikhs. Nor could they curtail re-

lations between chapters of Sufi brotherhoods situated within their territory and those located elsewhere. Islamic scholarship and piety did not march to the beat of the sultan's drum.

A crucial question for the future, therefore, is whether the nation-state has become so firmly established in the Muslim world as to set political limits on new efforts to credential religious authorities. Many of today's governments act as though they have such power. They try to limit the participation of religious activists in elections and in the direction of citizens' organizations like bar associations and student governments. Some of them also control the building of mosques, regulate the appointment of mosque officials, and dictate the texts of Friday sermons. In legal affairs, even a religious state like Iran has a national law code that does not apply beyond Iran's borders.

As against this evidence that religion is constrained by national borders, hundreds of Muslim organizations and movements operate in disregard of national boundaries. Some are highly publicized terrorist organizations like al-Qaeda. Some are welfare and service organizations that raise money abroad for relief of distress at home. Some are Sufi brotherhoods or other pious associations that have chapters in many lands. Some are formally international, like the various offshoots of the Organization of the Islamic Conference. And still others embody less formally the traditional commitment of Muslims to viewing their faith community as a single *umma*, and to looking to the tradition of a universal caliphate, with authority over all Muslims, as a live option for the future.

The tug-of-war between national and transnational expressions of Islam does not have an obvious resolution. If the nation-state should prove the stronger force, resolution of the crisis of authority could well involve organizational forms with little prior history in Islam, such as national councils of ulama, Islamic political parties operating within single states, state-regulated religious educational institutions, or even formal sectarian denominations with national officials. On the other hand, if the transnational tradition should win out, the sovereignty of the various Muslim nation-states, already under real or prospective assault by the new American imperialism, will suffer further erosion, possibly accompanied by rearrangements of state boundaries to fit religious trends.

In this whirlpool of possibilities, activities on the edge will warrant greater attention than those in the center. If history is any indicator, the current governments of Muslim states like Saudi Arabia, Egypt, and Pakistan will play minor roles in reconstructing Islam for the twenty-first century. The same may be said of the traditional centers of learning, whether large and famous seminaries like al-Azhar in Egypt, or "one room schoolhouses" like the *pesantrans* of Indonesia and *madrasas* of Pakistan. The creativity and vitality needed to effect change has come in the past from dynamic edge populations, not from the establishment.

Three edge situations will bear careful watching:

1.  Muslim diaspora communities in non-Muslim lands, primarily in Europe and America.
2.  Democratically oriented political parties in Muslim majority countries.
3.  Higher education, either private or governmental, in countries where seminaries of traditional type have lost their cachet, such as Turkey, or where they never had great importance, such as Indonesia.

Diaspora communities have a long history in Islam. Muslim voyagers were famous for establishing trading colonies that became the nuclei of more extended communities composed of both immigrants and local converts. Today's diasporas, however, are developing within new political, legal, and social situations. In the past, diasporas of all sorts tended to form inward looking communities. Political restrictions sometimes threatened a community's well-being, as did social and religious customs in the host country; but the anxieties raised by these threats helped the community maintain cohesion since people felt they had no one to rely on but themselves. Today, diaspora communities in Europe and America—as opposed to migrant labor communities in the Persian Gulf region—seek economic inclusion and legal normalization, and social assimilation is becoming increasingly attractive to diaspora born children. Maintaining community boundaries and preserving traditions from generation to generation becomes problematic in these situations. But the benefits offered by the promise of legal equality in the western secular democracies make this burden bearable. Diaspora leaders who expect to see their grandchildren living permanently in their host country accept the reality that they will never live under a government or legal system based on Islam. This assumption is clearly at odds with traditional interpretations of Islamic law, much of which is predicated on the existence of an Islamic state. This legal difference creates for the diaspora a unique edge situation. They need to figure out how to be Muslim and avoid a loss of Muslim identity under these conditions.

The attacks of 9/11 brought the dilemma of life in the Muslim diaspora into high relief, not just in the United States but in other countries as well. Arab intellectuals who once considered the distinction between Muslim and Christian irrelevant to their common nationalist interests began to see the world through religiously tinted lenses. Muslims from non-Arab lands began to discover that apprehensive non-Muslim host societies were paying less attention to language and ethnicity and more to the common profession of Muslim faith. And immigrant communities began to come closer to local groups of Muslim converts as both confronted the religiously based suspicions of non-Muslims. In short, talk about Islam in the diaspora became decidedly more intense and more anxious

Within the American and European diaspora communities, articulate and educated men and women abound. Since 9/11 they have taken the lead in appraising the problems of Muslims— whether in the diaspora, or in their countries of origin, or throughout the umma. Speaking out and writing constitute only one form of community leadership, however. An Egyptian émigré in France may offer an acute analysis of the Egyptian scene, but have little say about the conditions of Muslim life in France. A Moroccan theologian in California may publish a penetrating study of Quranic views on human rights, but regard it as pertinent to the umma as a whole rather than to his or her local Muslim community.

If the edge communities of the diaspora are to become the seedbeds of new approaches to authority, bridges will be needed between outspoken intellectuals and local community institutions. At present, this sort of coordination is more apparent in non-diasporic communities. In Muslim majority countries, intellectuals commonly work with, or try to form, political and social organizations. This is understandable inasmuch as government surveillance and restrictions, combined with government failures in the area of jobs and social services, invite social action and political organizing. Parties and movements in these countries, and the intellectuals that sympathize with them, shape their programs within, and as responses to, the limitations imposed by dictators, monarchs, and generals, with the implicit endorsement of the western governments that support them. By contrast, the diaspora communities generally work within contexts of legal freedom and constitutional equality, and their leaders focus more on sustaining community life and ensuring that legal rights are observed than on organizing to oppose tyranny. As a consequence, strong-minded diaspora intellectuals often find the local challenges less compelling than those posed by the plight of Muslims elsewhere.

Despite their intellectual energy and the freedom of expression they enjoy, diaspora communities illustrate in microcosm the broader problem of old authorities versus new authorities. Imams and community leaders resemble the old authorities of majority Muslim lands. But they enjoy greater respect because they have not been subjected to colonial domination or radical anticlerical pressures. These individuals gain authority through personal leadership and direct work within their communities, and they focus most of their attention on the problems of their own followers within the diaspora. The Muslim intellectuals and preachers whose voices are more frequently heard in the public arena represent the contrasting trend. They are new authorities insofar as they seek to influence people through ideas and arguments propounded in books and through the electronic media. They are more gratified by learning that their ideas have had an impact thousands of miles away than by gaining a respectful hearing in their local mosque.

All is not black and white, of course. Many individuals work within both realms. The problem with working within both realms, however, is finding a balance between what is meaningful for the diaspora and what is meaningful for Muslims elsewhere, whether in the intellectual's home country or in the umma more generally. One might envision diaspora communities building national organizational structures—the new national Muslim council in France comes to mind—and using those structures to assert control over who can speak authoritatively for Islam in the national diaspora community. But given the traditions of free speech in the secular western democracies, it is hard to see how such structures could hope to rein in the free-wheeling thoughts and writings of individual intellectuals.

Turning to the second important edge, the politically restless societies in the lands of tyranny, the problem of localism versus transnational tradition rears its head in a different fashion. Before 9/11, and despite the transnational propaganda for Islamic revolution that briefly followed the overthrow of the Shah in 1979, most religious activists couched their appeals in national terms and organized their political parties with a view to competing in national elections. The Muslim Brotherhood in Egypt, for example, was not the same as the Muslim Brotherhood in Jordan or in Kuwait. Since 9/11, however, the transnational appeal of a jihad of all Muslims against all of the enemies of Islam—rhetorically Jews and Crusaders, but stretching the terms to include Indians in Kashmir and Russians in Chechnya—has gained both publicity and headway. Enormous numbers of Muslims, frustrated by the military feebleness and domestic political oppression of their national governments, have come to agree with Osama bin Laden's geostrategic analysis and to respect the austere image he conveys of a selfless warrior for the faith. But his program of action has far less appeal, in large part because it has nothing to offer but death.

By projecting a global rather than a national scale for his jihad, Bin Laden excited an audience that had never imagined such boldness. Yet he also cut himself off from working within national political systems. Overthrowing the Egyptian or Saudi government might be an expedient tactic, but establishing Islam-friendly democracies in those countries would be no substitute for combating the Jews and Crusaders. For political vision, all he can offer is a vaguely articulated revival to the universal caliphate, an option whose hollowness became patent when he claimed that post for the religiously undistinguished leader of Afghanistan's Taliban regime.

Ideological alternatives that focus on working within national political systems have far greater long-term potential than anything that has so far materialized among the advocates of jihad. But most of those national alternatives, including the many that call for free elections, have been severely repressed by police state regimes. The result has been a classic example of empowering the violent extreme by crushing the nonviolent alternatives. Incorporating Islamic political movements and parties into liberalized political systems structured on open elections is the best tactic for undermining the appeal of transnational jihad.

Implementing a policy of this sort would put strong pressure on would-be participants in elections to move beyond the rousing but insubstantial rhetoric of mass mobilization to the proposal of specific governing programs. Successful programs would result in religious parties forming governments or gaining significant parliamentary influence, and this in turn would tend to cast any new structures of Islamic religious authority in nation-state molds since they would most likely be based on the platforms of the parties. As in other democratic systems, successful party leaders, in this case, of avowedly Islamic parties, would come to be viewed as authorities credentialed by popular electoral appeal. This might not make them truly religious authorities if they lacked spiritual stature or knowledge, but it would delegitimize ideologues committed to rejecting electoral institutions.

In principle, the role in of independent intellectuals in countries where Islamic parties actively participate in free elections should be similar to their role in the diaspora. (Some Muslim countries, of course, such as Jordan, Lebanon, Yemen, Malaysia, Pakistan, and Indonesia, permit religious parties to run for office at the present time. However, electoral laws and government control of broadcast media sometimes limit democratic freedom.) Ideally, they would be free to air their views and court audiences both within and beyond the national boundaries. But real politics tend to absorb intellectual energies. In all likelihood, intellectuals would tend to align themselves with one or another Islamic party, something they are not so likely to do in the diaspora. Given freedom of electoral participation, in other words, an Egyptian philosopher working in alignment with an Egyptian Islamic political party could hope to see his or her ideas contributing to new Egyptian realities. But a Muslim philosopher working in France can have few expectations, as a specifically Muslim voice, of effecting significant changes in French governing policies beyond those directly affecting the diaspora community.

Hypothetical situations neither predict nor shape the future. They are helpful, however, in highlighting the importance of scale in visualizing possible outcomes of Islam's crisis of authority. Islam is and will remain a faith based on a universal message and an indestructible sense of brotherhood across the broad expanse of the umma. Muslims will continue to draw inspiration from a glorious past and to keep alive the idea of the shari'a, the law of all Muslims. Yet people do not lead their lives at the universal level. Advocates of comprehensive change, whether they are calling for a reintroduction of ijtihad, or precise adherence to the practices of Muhammad and his Companions, or global jihad against Jews and Crusaders, may stimulate the mind or stir the blood, but politics are ultimately local. And politics in the American and European diaspora communities differ profoundly from those in Muslim majority states suffering under tyrannical rule. These two Muslim worlds have much to say to each other, but the circumstances of their respective worlds inhibit dialogue.

Ways of bridging the politics of local concern are sure to materialize, but it is hard to see them evolving either from Islamic political parties or from the preoccupation of diaspora communities with building Islam in their host countries. Hence my suggestion that the structures of higher education throughout the umma deserve scrutiny. Over the last two centuries, Islam's Christian sibling in the great Islamo-Christian civilization has seen the professoriat overtake the clergy as the most influential international body of authorities bound by common credentialing procedures. It is not at all impossible to envision a parallel development in twenty-first century Islam.

It is already the case that a substantial proportion of the new authorities that have gained national and transnational followings over the past forty years hold advanced degrees from secular institutions. Far from disguising this fact, they implicitly use it to enhance their appeal. Their degrees advertise that their religious thinking has not been shaped by a stifling and old-fashioned seminary curriculum, and they also mark them as leaders whose ability has been recognized—credentialed—even by people who care nothing for Islam. (A comparative census of successful Protestant evangelists in the United States—and probably of the U.S. Congress—would be hard pressed to find so high an average level of secular educational achievement.) An optimist might conclude from this that Muslims are yearning to follow people whose intelligence they respect, and that they are inclined to see educational attainment outside the seminary system as a respectable credential. A pessimist might respond that possession of an advanced degree in medicine, engineering, law, education, or economics does not qualify a person as a religious thinker and leader.

Though traditional seminaries are comparatively few, at the present time there are thousands of professors of Islamic law, Islamic theology, and Islamic missionary enterprise in universities of recognizable international form throughout the Muslim world. They train people to attend to the religious needs of Muslim communities at home and to spread sound Muslim practice in communities abroad. But in most Muslim countries, this religious professoriat is employed by state universities and thus subject to autocratic government control. For the professoriat to assert itself as a wellspring of religious authority that can compete with religious political parties and self-proclaimed renewers, a higher level of intellectual autonomy will be needed, something like the intellectual freedom enjoyed by the western professoriat—or the economic and curricular independence of the traditional seminaries before the era of modernization.

The Rector of the Syarif Hidayatullah State Islamic University in Jakarta, Azyumardi Azra, maintains that "*pesantren* [traditional religious schools] and Islamic universities [in Indonesia] are in fact turning out Muslims with moderate thoughts and strong religious tolerance because they perceive Islam as a social phenomenon." Extremists, he observes, are more likely to come from institutions with strong science programs, such as the University of Indonesia, the Bogor Institute of Agriculture and the Bandung Institute of Technology.[6]

Azyumardi Azra earned his doctoral degree at Columbia University under an Indonesian government program to encourage promising scholars of Islam to study in western secular universities rather than traditional centers of learning such as al-Azhar in Egypt. Many of his faculty have similar backgrounds. The head of al-Muhammadiyah, Indonesia's second largest Muslim organization, who completed his doctoral studies on Islam in the United States at the University of Chicago, concurs with Azyumardi Azra's analysis. The problem, he contends, is that the secular, science-oriented universities do not impart a sufficiently comprehensive understanding of Islam.

There is obviously something absurd about the implication that first-rate training in moderate and tolerant interpretations of Islam is best acquired at secular western universities. This absurdity encapsulates the educational dilemma, however. Higher education in the Muslim world divides into two tracks, one secular and the other religious. The secular track, which originated in the programs established by westernizing regimes in the nineteenth century to train government personnel, involves only limited religious training. Yet the most popular, outspoken, and innovative religious thinkers, including many who strongly advocate jihad and intolerance, come from this track. The religious track, which saw its financial independence and aura of authority undermined by those same governments, trains competent, and often moderate, specialists who resent the prominence of their less qualified rivals from secular institutions. But they generally lack both the societal respect and the intellectual freedom to make a significant public impact. Unfortunately, renewed respect for solid religious education, which might help alleviate the crisis of authority, runs counter to the anticlerical ideology of many Muslim governments, and to the secular spirit that generally underlies modern education worldwide.

Indonesia never developed a high-level religious educational network under Dutch colonial rule so it has been freer to experiment with Islamic education than countries with more entrenched educational traditions. Many major cities have a State Institute for Islamic Studies (IAIN), largely staffed by professors trained in Islamic studies in the West. Azyumardi Azra directs the first IAIN to be accorded university status. While this experiment may well remain confined to Indonesia, it shows that secular governments are not incapable of thinking creatively about the problem of religious authority if they are not burdened by fear of the ulama becoming once again a rival political force.

Diaspora communities, Islamic political parties, and university training in religion do not exhaust the list of edge situations from which institutional initiatives for change might develop. However, they serve to illustrate some of the problems that will have to be overcome as the world Muslim community confronts its crisis of authority. Given what Muslims have created from their religious tradition over the past fourteen centuries, I have no doubt whatsoever that solutions will be found. And I fully expect that the next twenty to thirty years will see religious leaders of tolerant and peaceful conscience, in the mold of Gandhi, Martin Luther King, and Nelson Mandela, eclipse in respect and popular following today's advocates of jihad, intolerance, and religious autocracy.

# Appendix on Quantitative Onomastics

THIS APPENDIX elaborates on the methodological aspects of the discussion of the popularity of male names on pages 76–78. Conferral of given names involves many influences that differ in particulars from family to family and child to child. Family custom, desire to preserve the name of a deceased relation, emulation of an esteemed public figure, and honoring a friend or mentor may all play a role. Yet however complex and personal factors of this sort may be, they tend to remain more or less constant over time and therefore to cancel one another out when large numbers of names are aggregated.

Other factors change systematically in response to parental expectations regarding the future. When parents think seriously about the kind of society in which their sons will live their lives, they give names that tacitly reflect that anticipation. In this way they reveal their individual appraisals of the trajectory of change they see around them. Since in most cultures parents still tend to see sons as likely autonomous actors in society, and daughters as living their lives within family units whose public identities will derive from male members, male naming betrays this factor of societal anticipation more surely than female naming.

As a benchmark for name change in a society making a transition from religious identity to secular identity, I have systematically extracted a sample of male names from the list of students graduating from Harvard College between 1671 and 1877. I have estimated birth-dates by subtracting 21 years from the date of graduation. Though none of the males involved was assured at birth of becoming a Harvard graduate, it is safe to presume that the parents who gave them their names were, or became during their sons' younger years, literate enough to value higher education; prosperous enough to spare their sons from laboring on the farm or in the workshop; and resident near enough to Boston, the Massachusetts colonial capital, to facilitate a son's sojourn in Cambridge on the other side of the Charles River. These considerations imply a measure of homogeneity with respect to social class, and this class identity in turn implies a relatively homogeneous worldview. Historians of colonial America agree that this worldview was dominated, at the outset of this period, by the strongly religious traditions of the Massachusetts Bay Colony.

Graph 1 (p. 76) records the change over time in the frequency of Harvard names drawn from the Old Testament. It dramatically illustrates both the strength of religious sensibility and the waning of that sensibility over time. In the earliest usable age cohort (1671), Old Testament names—e.g., Samuel, Nathaniel, Benjamin, Ezekiel—account for 40% of all names. This proportion rises to 45% by 1760. (By way of comparison, the names of early graduates of William and Mary College, in non-Puritan Virginia, show no particular bias toward Biblical models.) Then between 1760 and 1860, the rate of Old Testament naming falls to below 10%, where it steadily remains until Harvard expands the geographical and social scope of its undergraduate recruiting in the 1950s.

No special expertise in American history is needed to identify the point where the curve turns downward, particularly if one allows for the likelihood that many students of that era graduated from Harvard at a somewhat younger age than 21, which would put the inflection point of the curve a bit later than 1760.[1] The Seven Years War, known in North America as the French and Indian War, ended in 1763. Seeking to recoup its military expenditures, Britain immediately began to enforce the existing Navigation Laws and then imposed a series of new taxation measures—the Sugar Act (1764), the Quartering Act and Stamp Act (1765), the Townsend Acts (1767)—that bore heavily on the commercial class of a major port city like Boston. Thus were sown some of the seeds of the American Revolution.

Given the continuation of the decline in Biblical naming through and after the period of the revolution, it is hard to escape the conclusion that the tendency that set in during the 1760s had a good deal to do with the rising current of political tension and protonational identity that exploded into war in 1776 and gave birth to a new nation. Massachusetts citizens had lived their lives within the sound of their churchbells since the colony's founding by Puritan settlers. But now Boston became a hotbed of rebellion and agitation for a new national identity. In this climate, it is not surprising that more and more well-to-do parents anticipated that their sons would grow up in a public arena in which religion would play a diminishing role. This does not necessarily signal a decline in personal piety, only an increasing number of parents guessing that their sons would do better with a nonreligious name than a religious one. (Ironically, the names they initially turned to were the names of the English kings: Henry, Edward, George, etc.)

Now for a Muslim example: Turkish naming between 1820 and 1908. The names used to produce the curve on Graph 2 (p. 76) are the names of members of the Büyük Millet Meclisi, the parliament of the Turkish Republic established in 1921, along with the names of their fathers and the names of the members of the short-lived Ottoman Parliament of 1876. Birthdates are available for all three groups. The name set I have adopted as equivalent in the Ottoman cultural setting to Old Testament names in Massachusetts consists of three names associated with the person and family of the prophet Muhammad: Mehmet, Ahmet, and Ali. In terms of social class, it is obvious that these men came from families with sufficient money, prestige, and political awareness for them (or their sons) to stand for elective office. They represent, in other words, a stratum of elite families distributed across Turkey. (I have excluded non-Anatolian representatives from 1876.)

As with the Harvard names, religious names dominate the early onomasticon, the three under examination being borne by 30–35% of the group. In 1839 the curve abruptly reverses direction and continues steadily downward heading for a nadir of 7% during the Young Turk Revolution of 1908, with only one temporary recovery during the 1890s when Sultan-Caliph Abdülhamit II was actively promoting Pan-Islam and his own role as the paramount leader of the Muslim world. As for the cause of the dramatic downturn, a sudden crisis beset the Ottoman Empire in 1839. Muhammad Ali, the rebellious Ottoman governor of Egypt, had taken control of Syria in 1833. In 1839 his son Ibrahim invaded Anatolia and thrashed the newly reorganized army of Sultan Mahmud II. That same year, Mahmud's navy surrendered to Muhammad Ali at Alexandria, and Mahmud himself died. European intervention alone prevented the fall of Istanbul. In return, and in addition to the demands they made on Muhammad Ali, the Europeans sought far-reaching Europeanizing changes from Mahmud's son and successor, Sultan Abdülmecit. The sultan's highly publicized "reform" decree of 1839, the Imperial Rescript of the Rose Chamber, inaugurated the period of institutional change known as the Tanzimat ("Reorganization") during which European-style schools, law codes, and bureaucratic practices steadily replaced their traditional, religiously imbued counterparts. These changes affected most the stratum of elite families that subsequently emerged as the political class of the late empire and the subsequent Turkish Republic. It is from this stratum that the names are drawn.

It is hardly surprising that the families who were most aware of the Europeanizing aspirations of the Tanzimat's architects increasingly bestowed nonreligious names on their sons after 1839. Except during the brief flurry of Pan-Islamic sentiment stirred up by Sultan Abdülhamit II, the trajectory of Turkish public life that they saw evolving was distinctly one of assimilation to European values and practices, culminating in the revolution of 1908, which was initially hailed by politically aware Muslims, Christians, and Jews alike as a triumph of national over religious identity. (The social-psychological roots of Atatürk's subsequent success at formalizing secularism as the ideology of his Turkish Republic stand sharply revealed by this evolution in naming.)

Two case studies are not sufficient to validate an analytical technique, but the similarity between onomastic developments in societies as far removed from one another as eighteenth-century Massachusetts and nineteenth-century Turkey encourages a third comparison: naming in Iran. Work by Iranian sociologists studying the impact of the Iranian Revolution provides the data. Graph 5 summarizes some of the findings of these studies. Line A comes from Nader Habibi's study of Hamadan, a provincial capital.[2] It shows that a decline in the popularity of "Islamic" names prior to the 1970s reversed during the years immediately preceding the revolution of 1979 and then recommenced quite quickly after the establishment of the Islamic Republic. Over the period covered, 1962–1987, the decline in the inclination to bestow "Islamic" names exceeded 25%. Line B combines Ahmad Rajabzadeh's findings for Hamadan and Arak, another provincial city.[3] It is also the line shown on Graph 3 (p. 77). It shows "Islamic" naming accounting for between 70% and 80% of all names down to the mid-1930s. Then begins a marked decline that coincides chronologically with Reza Shah Pahlavi's promotion of Iranian nationalism as the state ideology and his efforts to suppress religious customs, most dramatically his 1936 prohibition on women wearing the *chador*. More and more parents opt for nonreligious names throughout the next three decades. Then the trend reverses in the prerevolutionary years of the mid-1970s. This brief resurgence of "Islamic" naming peaks around 1977, and then the decline resumes. By 1993 when the study ends, 44% fewer urban parents are choosing "Islamic" names for their children.

Questions of gender and of what constitutes an "Islamic" name complicate analysis of these findings. Rajabzadeh, for example, tabulates male and female names separately but does not break these tabulations down into rural and urban, as he does his more general figures. Abbas Abdi, in a study of children's naming in Tehran, addresses these problems.[4] However, drawing data from the national capital, where political currents are felt more acutely and with more volatile effect than in the provinces, adds further complications. Line C reflects his tabulation of "Islamic" naming

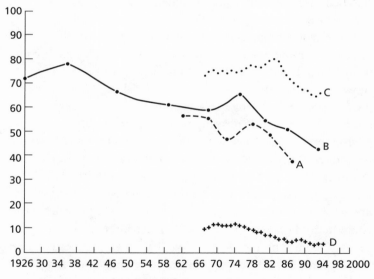

5 Frequency of Islamic names in Iran: **A** "Islamic" names from Hamadan (Habibi), **B** "Islamic" names from Hamadan and Arak (Rajabzadeh), **C** Combined "religious" names among boys in Tehran (Abdi), **D** "Customary religious" names among boys in Tehran (Abdi)

among boys. The numbers are substantially higher than those recorded by Habibi and Rajabzadeh, and the sharp decline that the other studies date to the onset of revolutionary activity in 1977–78 does not set in until 1983, possibly as a disillusioned reaction to the war with Iraq or the civil war between the government of the Islamic Republic and the Mojahedin-e Khalq. The decline remains steady after that, however, in consonance with the findings of Habibi and Rajabzadeh.

This summary presentation of the findings of three independent research projects does not do justice to the complexity of their work, but there would seem to be no doubt about their broad import. In religiously oriented societies, strong assertions of a collective identity divorced from religious affiliation trigger sharp declines in religious naming: the onset of republican revolutionary ferment in Massachusetts, imperial endorsement of Europeanizing changes in Turkey (the Ottoman Empire), and Reza Shah Pahlavi's highly publicized secularizing measures and advocacy of Iranian nationalism in Iran. As more and more parents begin to visualize a future in which public and political life does not revolve around religion, they signal their expectations of change in the names they bestow on their children. In the Iranian case, the decline briefly turned around in the mid-1970s as agitation against the Shah's rule acquired a strong religious complexion, just as it briefly turned around in Turkey when Abdülhamit II promoted Pan-Islam as an imperial ideology.

Graph 4 (p. 79) compares the rate of naming change in Iran with the rates in Turkey and Massachusetts. Setting equal at 100% the level of religious naming at the highwater points of the respective curves, 1760+, 1838, and 1936±, we can see how rapidly parents in the three different situations began to bestow other sorts of names. The points are plotted 10 years before the inflection point and then 10 years after, 20 years after, 30 years after, etc. The Turkish sample shows the most rapid decline in religious naming, at least down to the brief recovery in the Hamidian period. The skewing of the sample toward elite and politically aware families may account for this. As for the curves for Massachusetts and for the provincial Iranian cities of Arak and Hamadan, they virtually coincide up until the short-lived reversal of the Iranian trend before the 1979 revolution. The rate of decline subsequent to the revolution is slightly steeper than that in Massachusetts.

# Notes

## 1. Islamo-Christian Civilization

1. New York: Friendship Press, 1926.
2. Ibid., p. 41.
3. Ibid., p. 196.
4. Ibid., pp. 216–18.
5. Boston: Houghton Mifflin, 1923.
6. *Decline and Fall of the Roman Empire* (New York: Bradley, nd, vol. V, p. 423).
7. John W. Bohnstedt, *The Infidel Scourge of God: The Turkish Menace as Seen by German Pamphleteers of the Reformation Era*, Transactions of the American Philosophical Society, N.S. LVIII/9 (1968), p. 44.
8. Jacob R. Marcus, ed., *The Jew in the Medieval World: A Source Book, 315–1791*, (1938; reprint, Westport: Greenwood, 1975, p. 45).
9. Prudence Jones and Nigel Pennick, *A History of Pagan Europe* (London: Routledge, 1995, pp. 92–93).

## 2. What Went On?

1. *What Went Wrong? Western Impact and Middle Eastern Response* (Oxford: Oxford University Press, 2002), p. 3.
2. *The Emergence of Modern Turkey*, 3rd ed. (Oxford: Oxford University Press, 2002), pp. ix–x.

3. Ibid.
4. Ibid.
5. Second ed., Cairo: al-Hilal, 1899. I discovered this hitherto unnoticed work in a box of books being discarded by Columbia University's law library. I am deeply grateful to Muhammad Kassab for many fruitful discussions we had of its contents.
6. Pp. 4–6.
7. Ibid.
8. Halil Inalcik, *The Ottoman Empire: The Classical Age 1300–1600* (New York: Praeger, 1973), p. 66.
9. *What Went Wrong?*, p. 54.
10. Bryan Turner, *Weber and Islam*, (London: Routledge & Kegan Paul, 1978).
11. Printing in the Arabic script developed earlier among Arab Christians, but this seems to have had little impact on their Muslim neighbors.

## 3. Looking for Love in All the Wrong Places

1. For information on this obscure episode, in which I was personally involved, see "CBS Evacuates from the Quagmire that was 'Saigon,'" *Los Angeles Herald Examiner*, Oct. 22, 1985.
2. Martin Kramer, *Ivory Towers on Sand: The Failure of Middle East Studies in America* (Washington, D.C.: The Washington Institute for Near East Policy, 2001, pp. 5–11).
3. Operations Coordinating Board, Washington, D.C., *Inventory of U.S. Government and Private Organization Activity Regarding Islamic Organizations as an Aspect of Overseas Operations,* May 3, 1957 (declassified 1991), pp. 1–2. My thanks to Charles Kurzman and Herb Klagsbrun for drawing my attention to this document
4. Ibid., p. 4–5.
5. Ibid., pp. 5–6.
6. Ibid., p. 9.
7. Ibid., p.14–15.
8. Kramer, *Ivory Towers on Sand*, p. 13.
9. Daniel Lerner, *The Passing of Traditional Society: Modernizing the Middle East* (New York: The Free Press, 1958). The questionnaire is contained in Appendix A.
10. Ibid., p. 82.

11. Ibid., p. 13

12. Ibid., p. 83.

13. Ibid., p. 47.

14. Carleton S. Coon, *Caravan: The Story of the Middle East* (New York: Holt, Rinehart, and Winston, 1951).

15. Lerner, *The Passing of Traditional Society,* p. 409.

16. Ibid., p. xii–xiii.

17. Ibid., p. 51–52.

18. Ibid., pp. 33–34.

19. Ibid., pp. 34.

20. Ibid., chap. 7–8.

21. John C. Campbell, *Defense of the Middle East: Problems of American Policy* (New York: Harper,1958).

22. Ibid., p. 367.

23. Ibid., p. 298.

24. Shoshanah Haberman, ed., "Special Policy Forum Report: Combating the Ideology of Radical Islam," The Washington Institute of Near East Policy, Policywatch #746, April 10, 2003. I am grateful to Barak Barfi for bringing this report to my attention.

25. Campbell, p. 361–2.

26. John Brown, "The Purposes and Cross-Purposes of American Public Diplomacy," p. 6. www.unc.edu/depts/archives_roll/2002_07–09/brown_pubdipl/brown_pubdipl.html.

27. Ibid., p. 8.

28. Speech at UCLA on April 2, 2003; adapted and distributed by Global Viewpoint on April 3, 2003 as "This Is World War IV."

29. Nader Fergany, et al., *Arab Human Development Report 2002,* New York: United Nations Development Programme, Regional Bureau for Arab States (RBAS), 2002, p. 2.

30. Ibid., pp. 8–9.

31. Haberman, op. cit., note 24.

32. Ibid.

33. Ibid.

## 4.  The Edge of the Future

1. New York: Columbia University Press

2. Manjhan, *Madhumalati: An Indian Sufi Romance*, tr. Aditya Behl and Simon Weightman, Oxford: Oxford University Press, 2000,

pp. 1, 5. I wish to thank Prof. Frances Pritchett for introducing me to this text.

3. For northeast India, this historical situation is described in detail in Richard Eaton, *The Rise of Islam and the Bengal Frontier, 1204–1760* (Berkeley: University of California Press, 1993).

4. John R. Bowen, *Muslims Through Discourse* (Princeton: Princeton University Press, 1993).

5. Ibid., p. 202–3.

6. Muhammad Nafik, "US Anti Terrorist Aid Should Help Moderates Not Military," *Jakarta Post* (August 6, 2002) www.globalpolicy.org/wtc/targets/2002/0806jakarta.htm

## Appendix on Quantitative Onomastics

1. Cotton Mather graduated in 1678 at age 15, Increase Mather in 1656 at 17, John Adams in 1755 at 20.

2. Nader Habibi, "Popularity of Islamic and Persian Names in Iran before and after the Islamic Revolution," *International Journal of Middle East Studies*, vol. 24 (1992), examines a sample of names given to children in the city of Hamadan between 1962 and 1987.

3. Ahmad Rajabzadeh's *Tahlil-e Ijtima'i-ye Namgozari* ("The Social Analysis of Name-giving," Tehran, 1999) provides a more extensive and complex study of names bestowed in the provincial cities of Hamadan, Arak, and Bushehr between 1921 and 1995. He analyzes rural patterns for those areas separately and finds them to be more conservative. I have left out his findings from Bushehr because they are complicated by different practices among Persian-speaking parents and Arabic-speaking parents.

4. Abbas Abdi, *Tahavol-e Namgozari-ye Kudakan-e Tehrani* ("The Transformation of Name-giving of Tehran Children," Tehran, 1999), covers the period 1966 to 1995.

# Works Cited

Abdi, Abbas. *Tahavol-e Namgozari-ye Kudakan-e Tehrani* ("The Transformation of Name-giving of Tehran Children") Tehran, 1999.

Bohnstedt, John W. *The Infidel Scourge of God: The Turkish Menace as Seen by German Pamphleteers of the Reformation Era*. Transactions of the American Philosophical Society, N.S. LVIII/9 (1968).

Bowen, John R. *Muslims Through Discourse*. Princeton: Princeton University Press, 1993.

Brown, John. "The Purposes and Cross-Purposes of American Public Diplomacy," p. 6. www.unc.edu/depts/archives_roll/2002_07–09/brown_pubdipl/brown_pubdipl.html.

Bulliet, Richard W. *Islam: The View from the Edge*. New York: Columbia University Press, 1994.

Bushtali, Yusuf. *Hidyat al-Muluk fi Adab al-Suluk* ("The Conduct of Kings on the Propriety of Behavior") 2nd ed., Cairo: al-Hilal, 1899.

Campbell, John C. *Defense of the Middle East: Problems of American Policy*. New York: Harper, 1958.

Coon, Carleton S. *Caravan: The Story of the Middle East*. New York: Holt, Rinehart, and Winston, 1951.

Eaton, Richard. *The Rise of Islam and the Bengal Frontier, 1204–1760*. Berkeley: University of California Press, 1993.

Fergany, Nader, et al. *Arab Human Development Report 2002*. New York: United Nations Development Programme, Regional Bureau for Arab States (RBAS), 2002.

Gibbon, Edward. *Decline and Fall of the Roman Empire*. New York: Bradley, nd.

Haberman, Shoshanah, ed. "Special Policy Forum Report: Combating the Ideology of Radical Islam." The Washington Institute of Near East Policy, Policywatch #746, April 10, 2003.

Habibi, Nader. "Popularity of Islamic and Persian Names in Iran before and after the Islamic Revolution." *International Journal of Middle East Studies*, vol. 24 (1992).

Halil Inalcik. *The Ottoman Empire: The Classical Age 1300–1600*. New York: Praeger, 1973.

Jones, Prudence and Nigel Pennick. *A History of Pagan Europe*. London: Routledge, 1995.

Kramer, Martin. *Ivory Towers on Sand: The Failure of Middle East Studies in America*. Washington, D.C.: The Washington Institute for Near East Policy, 2001.

Lerner, Daniel. *The Passing of Traditional Society: Modernizing the Middle East*. New York: The Free Press, 1958.

Lewis, Bernard. *The Emergence of Modern Turkey*, 3rd ed. Oxford: Oxford University Press, 2002.

Lewis, Bernard. *What Went Wrong? Western Impact and Middle Eastern Response*. Oxford: Oxford University Press, 2002.

Manjhan. *Madhumalati: An Indian Sufi Romance*, tr. Aditya Behl and Simon Weightman. Oxford: Oxford University Press, 2000.

Marcus, Jacob R., ed. *The Jew in the Medieval World: A Source Book, 315–1791*, 1938; reprint. Westport: Greenwood, 1975.

Mathews, Basil. *Young Islam on Trek: A Study in the Clash of Civilizations* New York: Friendship Press, 1926.

Operations Coordinating Board. Washington, D.C. *Inventory of U.S. Government and Private Organization Activity Regarding Islamic Organizations as an Aspect of Overseas Operations*, May 3, 1957.

Rajabzadeh, Ahmad. *Tahlil-e Ijtima'i-ye Namgozari* ("The Social Analysis of Name-giving"), Tehran, 1999.

Toynbee, Arnold. *The Western Question in Greece and Turkey: A Study in the Contact of Civilizations*. Boston: Houghton Mifflin, 1923.

Turner, Bryan. *Weber and Islam*. London: Routledge & Kegan Paul, 1978.

Woolsey, James. "This Is World War IV." *Global Viewpoint*, April 3, 2003.

# Index